Praise for *Andy Kaufman*

"Bob Zmuda connects on so many levels with this gripping yet hilarious inside industry chronicle. A great story of unconditional friendship and love framed in a studied portrait of a fascinatingly complex, brilliant, unduplicable anti-performance artist who may well resurrect to blow our minds again."

—Dan Aykroyd

"Danger. What would've or WILL Andy do next???? We wondered every time we saw him on TV or live on stage. I still wonder. We still laugh. The definition of an enigma, LIKE NO OTHER."

—Kathy Griffin

"I never worked with Andy Kaufman and I never even watched *Taxi*. I do like the name Andy, if that's any help."

—Paula Poundstone

"Bob Zmuda was (is?) Andy Kaufman's partner in all of Andy's reality-bending adventures. Is Andy's death yet another elaborate hoax by the ultimate performance artist? An absolutely astonishing read, *Andy Kaufman: The Truth, Finally* reveals all. Prepare to be amazed!"

—John Landis

"I was so fascinated by the melding of Andy's and Zmuda's mind that I spent two years of my life making a movie about it."

—Milos Forman

Andy

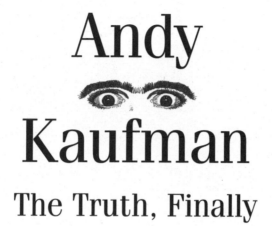

Kaufman

The Truth, Finally

Bob Zmuda
and
Lynne Margulies

BenBella Books, Inc.
Dallas, Texas

BenBella

BenBella Books, Inc.
10300 N. Central Expressway
Suite #530
Dallas, TX 75231
www.benbellabooks.com
Send feedback to feedback@benbellabooks.com

Printed in the United States of America
10 9 8 7 6 5 4 3 2 1

Library of Congress Cataloging-in-Publication Data
Zmuda, Bob, 1949-
  Andy Kaufman: the Truth, Finally / Bob Zmuda, Lynne Margulies.
    pages cm
  Includes bibliographical references and index.
    ISBN 978-1-940363-05-9 (hardback)—ISBN 978-1-940363-06-6 (electronic) 1. Kaufman, Andy, 1949-1984. 2. Comedians—United States—Biography. 3. Television actors and actresses—United States—Biography. I. Margulies, Lynne Elaine, 1957- II. Title.
    PN2287.K28Z74 2014
    792.702'8092—dc23

                                                                        2014014709

Editing by Glenn Yeffeth and
    Katie Kennedy
Copyediting by Brian Buchanan
Text design by Publishers' Design
    and Production Services, Inc.

Proofreading by James Fraleigh
    and Jenny Bridges
Cover design by Sarah Dombrowsky
Text composition by Integra Software
    Services Pvt. Ltd
Printed by Lake Book Manufacturing

Distributed by Perseus Distribution
www.perseusdistribution.com

To place orders through Perseus Distribution:
Tel: (800) 343-4499
Fax: (800) 351-5073
E-mail: orderentry@perseusbooks.com

Significant discounts for bulk sales are available. Please contact Glenn Yeffeth at glenn@benbellabooks.com or (214) 750-3628.

Dedicated to

Stanley Kaufman
and
Chester Zmuda

Two fathers who created two troublemakers

Contents

Foreword

I t is an honor to write the foreword to this book for my good friend
Bob Zmuda. Not many people know this, probably because
they don't care, but I got my first job in show business from Bob
Zmuda. In 1986, I was a freshman at the University of Southern
California where I was studying screenwriting. One day I was
watching a show like *Entertainment Tonight* and saw Bob Zmuda
holding a press conference where he was announcing the forma-
tion of Comic Relief, an organization which was about to put on
a Live Aid–type event starring the world's greatest comedians to
benefit homeless health care centers across America.

At the time I had no interest in charity but I was obsessed
with comedy, so I called the offices of Comic Relief immediately
and told them I would love to volunteer and be a part of their
new organization. I think they just recently got phones and didn't
really have an infrastructure, so they kind of blew me off. I was
bummed because I could feel that this was going to be special. I
had just watched Live Aid the year before while bussing tables at
El Torito on Long Island, and the idea that all of my idols would
be performing on one show was almost more than I could handle.

A few months later, I got a call from a man named Jacques
Fiorentino who had come up with this idea with Bob, who said
they needed help, and would I be willing to help them produce a
series of smaller Comic Relief events at comedy clubs around the
country. I was in! And for the next half decade I worked at Comic
Relief for no pay and then for a little pay, producing benefits that
raised over a million dollars for the homeless.

Those years working with Jacques Fiorentino, Bob Zmuda, Mario Bernheim, Paul Bennett, Caroline Thompson, and so many others were magical. I remember when I was told I could attend rehearsals for the show and then got to sit in the Universal Amphitheatre watching Robin Williams, Billy Crystal, and Whoopi Goldberg run through the show for the crew. I do not think I have had a more exciting comedy nerd moment since. On the nights of the big shows, I gave myself the job of being the one who had to walk up to every comedian on the lineup and have them sign fifty posters, which we sold for the charity. That gave me an excuse to have five minutes to talk with every comedian I had ever dreamed of speaking to—everyone from Pee Wee Herman and Sam Kinison, to George Carlin and Harold Ramis. I still have some of those posters!

As the years went by, I became more involved in the charity side of Comic Relief and was inspired by the tireless work that people around the country do to help the homeless receive much needed health care and other vital services. Dennis Albaugh ran the charity side of Comic Relief and was a real angel who taught me the importance trying to lift up those who are in need. He died way too soon of cancer and I think about his wisdom and his big heart constantly.

When dealing with Bob, there was always the specter of Andy Kaufman. I was a fan of Andy's since I was a little kid and had watched almost all of his TV appearances religiously since I was in elementary school. I remember knowing that this comedian who I loved was about to be on a new show called *Taxi*. My aunt Sam was friends with one of the stars of *Friday's* (an ABC sketch show), and I recall sitting up one night watching the wheels come off the cart when Andy hosted and let a sketch collapse on live television, resulting in a fist fight. I am still confused about who was and who wasn't in on it.

Over the years I have forced Bob to tell me so many of the epic Andy Kaufman stories. I was able to spend a lot of time with Bob when he was working with Milos Forman and Jim Carrey on the biopic of Andy, *Man on the Moon*. Jim Carrey dreamed of getting this role, and I was with him running the camera when he made a video-taped audition at his home in character as Andy. When it was time to research the role, I traveled with Jim and visited Andy's childhood home on Long Island, his grave, and met with his brother Michael and his father to talk about Andy and the film.

I remember Andy's dad, Stanley, telling us he never understood what Andy was going through as a high school student in the nineteen sixties. They just didn't understand each other and fought a lot. Andy was experimenting with drugs and was opening his mind to arts of all kinds. He told us that one day Andy gave him a copy of Jack Kerouac's *On the Road* and asked him to read it.

He said one afternoon he was reading it in his bedroom and was crying because he finally understood his son and what he was going through and inspired by, when suddenly Andy entered the room. He said they talked and cried and connected, and then sat there reading passages of the book to each other.

I felt privileged to watch Bob and these brilliant people talk about how they would approach making this important film. On several occasions, I went to visit the set and Jim would only speak to me as Andy or Tony Clifton. It was really uncomfortable because Jim and I are good friends, but it was also truly hilarious. I was there to see Jerry Lawler recreate the terrifying pile driver moment on Jim in front of a huge stadium of fans.

I was so glad to see the film come out so well and be such a monument to Andy's work and the world's love of him. He continues to inspire people to this day, but there will never be anyone quite like him. Not even close.

I am thrilled that Bob has chosen to write books about his time with Andy and the years since his death. As a comedy student, there is no end to my interest in all of the old stories and I think it is important that we keep his memory alive so people will continue to go on YouTube or where ever else people go these days and hunt down all of the wonderful, insane comedy moments that Andy and Bob created.

I also want to thank Bob for giving me my first job in comedy. He allowed me to enter a world I had dreamed of being a part of since I was ten and was always warm and kind to me, even when I was little runt who he should have mistreated and abused.

So enjoy this book and, if it makes you happy, send some money to homeless health care organizations in your town. I am sure Andy wouldn't mind.

—Judd Apatow

National Health Care for the Homeless Council: www.nhchc.org

Health Care for the Homeless Inc.: www.hchmd.org

National Association of Community Health Centers: www.nachc.com

Alameda County Health Care for the Homeless: www.acphd.org

Introduction

P robably no performer in the last four decades has been shrouded in more mystery than the enigma known as Andy Kaufman. Andy wanted it that way, and I, as his writer and best friend, along with Lynne Margulies, the love of his life, have dutifully supported those wishes over all these years. But now that his artistic legacy is forever finally secure and our own mortal coil may be unraveling sooner than we ever expected, it's time for the truth to be finally told. And in Andy Kaufman's case, that truth is even stranger than fiction.

Between Lynne and myself, we have over seventy years of firsthand knowledge of Andy. We have read just about every article ever written about him and spoken often to all those closest to him.

As you will see, we hold nothing back. Lynne reveals for the first time that Andy was bisexual and possibly died of AIDS. I know for a fact that he faked his death and will be returning. Either of these opinions is both shocking and explosive.

So sit back, pour yourself a glass of milk, open a bag of chocolate chip cookies, and read the true account of Andrew Geoffrey Kaufman. And may his life (or supposed death) be a testament to all avant-garde artists everywhere never to give up their vision, no matter how unusual that vision may be.

—Bob Zmuda

I'll never forget it. I was on a T.M. course in Switzerland. There were about forty of us all sitting in the lotus position outside on a beautiful day, gathered around the Maharishi. He was lecturing. Occasionally, someone would ask him a question. I was still pretty shy back then. It took me a while to muster enough courage to raise my hand.

"Yes, Andy!"

"Maharishi, what is the secret of comedy?"

"The secret of comedy is ..."

He lowered his head, which he would do when he was giving something great thought. Paused ... then raised his head back up and with a broad smile on his face said: "Timing!"

We all laughed.

—ANDY KAUFMAN

CHAPTER 1

"I Am Not a Comedian"

Phone rings …

B: Hello?

A: Bob!

B: Yeah, Andy.

A: How would I go about getting my hands on a cadaver without anyone knowing?

B: Go dig one up, like Igor did.

A: Seriously, I'm not joking.

B: Neither am I. You could probably buy one from a city morgue some place. They routinely sell those poor homeless bastards to medical schools so med students can practice on them. But there's going to be paperwork. Besides, you need a body that looks like you—that complicates the matter.

A: Well, I'm kind of figuring that one out. If I died in a car crash or fire, that would make it harder to identify the body.

B: Yes, that's true, but they're still going to check dental records. How are you going to get around that?

A: Maybe I can have some of my teeth pulled out and throw them in the fire. Will that do?

B: You'll have to yank a hell of a lot of them out. They usually have X-rays of the entire set of teeth, uppers and lowers.

A few weeks later. Ring…

B: Hello Andy, what's up?

A: I figured it out!

B: Figured what out?

A: I don't go the cadaver route. I work with a real live body. I find someone who's dying of some disease, like cancer. At the end, they're all shrunken up and the chemotherapy makes them lose all their hair.

B: OK so far. I'm with you.

A: Bob, it's just what we did with Clifton. We made everyone think that you were me as Tony through prosthetics. I do kind of the same thing, but this time I find somebody who kind of resembles me who's terminal. I'll pay them off. This way, they can leave a substantial amount of money for their loved ones. And then on my end, I'll start to look like them.

B: How you gonna do that?

A: I'll lose weight. Shave my head. Maybe I'll even go through chemo myself. I wonder how much of that stuff a healthy person can take without doing too much damage to themselves. My hair will really fall out and I'll have severe weight loss. Everyone will really think I'm dying. Nobody has ever gone this far to pull something like this off. It would be the crowning achievement of my career.

B: What career? You'll be dead.

A: Exactly. Dead, but not forgotten. Eventually I'll come back.

B: Andy, are you serious about this?

A: Dead serious.

*   *   *

Lynne

Every time Andy would go to a doctor, he'd ask him if he had cancer. I'd get so mad at him, I'd say, "Andy, you're going to talk yourself into getting cancer." So he called me from the doctor's office one day and told me he had cancer. He said in a bragging tone, "You see, I told you I was going to get cancer." His doctors sat us down over the first week and said, "There's nothing we can do. You might not even live for six months. You're going to die."

The amazing thing is Andy took it like somebody had just told him he couldn't go to the movies—"Oh, all right." It's like he believed in magic or something and he'd be cured.

I think he was so evolved because of meditation that the thought of death didn't scare him. He didn't want to die. He just wasn't afraid of it. Then off we went to the Philippines to see this "psychic surgeon," getting two treatments a day, six days a week. You'd take off all your clothes except your underwear and then lie on a table. It's very sterile and you're in this third world country. It's very hot. And the décor is kind of bamboo fake Jesus. And you're standing in line with these Japanese tourists who come there on tour because it's a fun thing to do. So you have them, and then also a few people like Andy who are really very sick. So you lie on the table and the guy starts putting his little hands on you, and blood starts flowing out, and he starts pulling these gut-like things out of you. It only takes a few seconds and then they wipe you up and off you go, and then the next Japanese tourist lies down. So there we were for six weeks. Andy was good at first. But then around the time Bob got there, he turned for the worse and couldn't even walk. Bob had to go to some Catholic hospital and get down on his hands and knees and pray with the nuns before they would give him this World War II walker that was like a huge cage for Andy. Then back to LA in Cedars-Sinai Hospital. It's like he went to sleep and that was it.

When Andy died, many people thought he had faked his death. What the public didn't know is that for many years he had talked about faking his own death. The first person I know of who he told was John Moffitt, the producer of "Fridays," back in 1981. I know he talked to Bob about it constantly. He talked to me about it many times. He told his manager, George Shapiro. He also told an ex-girlfriend named Mimi. He told all of us he was serious about doing it and then he died. I was in the room the moment he passed, and yet at times I say to myself, Could he possibly have faked it? 'Cause if he had, he would have taken it all the way with his family, his loved ones being around the bed. He would have taken it that far. He would have done it to me.

*   *   *

If I had lectured him back in the States about crossing his t's and dotting his i's in regard to making those around him believe he was dying, once in the Philippines he took the task to heart. When I arrived in Baguio City, Philippines, on April 7, 1984, he totally appeared as someone who would be dead in a short time. He was skin and bones. He could hardly walk. Lynne would have to assist him going to the bathroom, clean him up and help him back into bed. It was truly a sad, pathetic sight worthy of an Academy Award. I was quite impressed. I couldn't wait to speak to him privately, but Lynne never left his side. Occasionally he would weep about his condition. I had only one opportunity to talk to him alone. He had fallen asleep and Lynne momentarily left the room to get a Coke from a machine down the hall. I jumped up and approached his bed. I shook him ever so gently and whispered, "Andy, wake up. It's Bob." He didn't stir. I shook him harder. He slowly started to wake. "I want to talk to you. Lynne's going to be back any minute." He began to come around, his eyes flickered and then opened. I said, "Andy, you with this dying routine…It's fantastic. Totally believable." He smiled softly and then said in a raspy, low-energy voice, "I'm really dying, Bob." I heard the key jiggle in the lock. Lynne had returned. I quickly ran back to the couch and picked up the paper as if I was reading it. Lynne entered the room. "How's he doing?" "Still sleeping, I guess."

He supposedly died at 6:20 p.m. on May 16, 1984. I was not bedside when he died. I had gone home for a few hours to sleep when I got the call from his secretary, Linda Mitchell. She simply said, "It's over." I hung up the phone and said to myself, "Over? … We've only just begun." I flew to the funeral in Great Neck a couple of days later. At the funeral, I had to try my best not to laugh out loud. Luckily, a stifled laugh with a little cough thrown in can appear as a sob. So now the long wait would start, year after year after year would pass. Surely he'd try somehow to get in contact with me. I certainly would receive some sign, something that only I would understand and could never be linked back to him. But nothing. Cold silence. Eventually, over time, I too believed he had died. He had to. Yes, he told me he was going to fake his death, but ten, twenty, twenty-five years later? It just had to be the most unimaginable coincidence ever. Had to be. Who plans to fake his death one day and then the next day really dies? It just doesn't happen, but it did. And it happened to the strangest individual who ever lived. And I believed his death like a fool. Against all odds believed it. Believed it because Andy wanted me to believe it. It's just like I told him, "You're going to have to convince me you died," and he did. But no more. So why did I change my mind? Facts, pure and simple. If you look at all the facts, you can only draw one conclusion: Andy Kaufman faked his own death.

*　　*　　*

It seems that so many critics and fans are driven almost to the point of distraction trying to break through the Kaufman enigma. You can only imagine the questions Lynne and I fielded for years, with people wondering what he was really like. Of course, one could never answer that. Can one answer that for anyone? Do we really know what made Abe Lincoln tick? Can Daniel Day Lewis tell us? Can anybody really explain you to anyone else? I'd venture to say you couldn't even explain yourself to yourself if you tried. Yet over the years, so many people (bright people) are still trying to figure Kaufman out. Intellectual thought falls short. But if there is one thing family and friends can agree on, it's the fact that he was strange, very strange. Perhaps the closest we can get to understand Kaufman is through his adherence to transcendental meditation, sex, fun, and metaphysics in no particular order. Don't fool yourself into thinking that an understanding of Andy is going to be easy. After all, his is the trigonometry of psyches. Things will not be black or white even though I will attempt at times to paint them as such, more for my own sanity than the reader's. Writing about madness hopefully needn't make the writer mad.

And also throw out all that comedy bullshit. I'm telling you, he was not a comedian and really shouldn't be judged through the prism of comedy, or you'll never come close to understanding him. Andy was funny (sometimes) because he was an absurdist, but being funny truly wasn't a goal. Remember, Andy wasn't waiting for the laughs. If they came, OK. He'd take them. But if they didn't—and many times they didn't—it really made no difference to him. It might have mattered to the TV executives, his managers, club owners, and the public, but to Andy, never. Laughter? How trite.

If he wasn't a comedian, then what was he? To me, Andy was a behavioral scientist. He was constantly measuring people's reaction to stimuli. Andy instinctively knew back in '72 what neuroscientists have recently discovered: that laughter is one way the brain deals with the discomfort of an embarrassing situation (Foreign Man), inappropriate jokes (Tony Clifton), or the surprise of an unexpected punch line ("Take my wife . . . please take her."). He was always looking at the human condition and poking his nose around in areas where no one else did. Who interviews a girl with a tape recorder right after he has sex with her for the first time, asking why she doesn't like to have her legs up high while she's having intercourse with him? Who would ask such a thing? The sex researcher Alfred Kinsey perhaps, but even Kinsey would be more demure about it and have the young lady fill out a questionnaire. Not Andy, because Andy doesn't care what she answers. That's irrelevant. What fascinates him is her shock at his asking. That's the behavior he's interested in exploring—the "uncomfortableness" of a situation. This is the behavior he would explore time and time again.

When he first started doing the Foreign Man act, which he lifted from seeing a Pakistani man telling bad jokes at Café Wha? in Greenwich Village when he was fourteen, he could see how painful it was for the man not getting laughs (even though Andy and a friend were dying inside). So Andy used that same uncomfortableness to his advantage. You were uncomfortable watching his Foreign Man character's ineptitude. The uncomfortableness led to nervous and embarrassed laughter from the audience. Andy milked that embarrassed laughter and accused the audience of "laughing at me, not with me." And then he would start to cry. This would only cause the audience to laugh louder. Occasionally there'd be a few sensitive people in the audience (usually women) who would get very offended at the audience for laughing at this poor soul (not knowing the whole thing was a put-on).

Andy would also utilize real situations from his own life, no matter how painful, and present them onstage. Sometimes they got people to laugh. Sometimes they got people angry. Sometimes they got an audience to walk out. To Andy, it was all the same. He just wanted real emotions. He wanted his audience to be in the *present*. When he ran into me in '74, I was fresh out of guerrilla street theater and radical Abbie Hoffman-style politics—fused with an almost unrelenting devotion to psychologist Abraham Maslow's theory of "self-actualization" and a living-in-the-*present* philosophy—and Andy and I immediately clicked. It was uncanny how we thought exactly alike. In interviews he would state, "Once I met Bob, I just knew he had to be my writer. We just looked at the world the same way."

Never forget that Kaufman's psychological imperative onstage was to search for the "uncomfortableness" in every situation. This bloodletting, like the Stations of the Cross, led him on the road to spiritual enlightenment. Performance would therefore become a sacred ritual, performance as High Mass. Fame and fortune would bring him comfort and security. Andy, on the other hand, would rather be uncomfortable and insecure and not a prisoner to the karma of the material world. As you will see, give him the opportunity to sabotage his career and he'd leap at it. When Dick Ebersol, producer of *Saturday Night Live,* designed a vote to banish him from SNL, it was just too tantalizing for Andy not to go along with it. His deep-rooted martyr complex couldn't be happier! Jesus had his Judas. Kaufman had his Ebersol. Judas and Ebersol have their roles to play in order for both narcissists to reach transcendence.

Andy was in heaven (not that the vote didn't hurt him—it did—deeply, which he also enjoyed). But at the same time it gave him fodder for his next scenario to act out. Andy is kicked out of show business. How uncomfortable is that! How embarrassing. Christ, it's another Everest to climb.

In this context, the ultimate scenario, Kaufman faking his death, is par for the course. Andy endures the crucifixion and martyrdom and all the benefits that go along with it. "They'll see how much they miss me when I'm gone." But like they said in the film *Man on the Moon,* it's a showbiz death in a showbiz town in a showbiz hospital. No one really dies. Not really! What fun!

The petty squabbles that people would get into would also fascinate him. He'd love to get people all riled up, taking the bait, and watch them go to pieces. And then he'd laugh, much as we would viewing a box full of puppies romping, biting, or tumbling over one another.

Andy was above the fray, not in an arrogant way, but more in an innocent way. He was probably one of the most innocent people I've ever known, at least in the beginning. But remember, we're talking forty to forty-five years ago. He existed smack in the middle of the '60s. Remember the flower children? Andy surrounded himself with them. It's been pointed out, most recently by writer Vernon Chatman, who just spent three years editing Andy's micro-cassette tapes of over eighty hours for Drag City's *Andy and His Grandmother* album, that Andy lacked cynicism. Vernon could not "detect one ounce of cynicism in Kaufman—none." Correctly so. And yet cynicism, like pain, can protect us from hurt. Put your hand in a fire, you quickly withdraw it. The pain protects you from more injury. So too cynicism protects us from the pain of society. Yes, it makes us jaded, but it constantly reminds us that there is a real cruel world out there.

Because Andy didn't have that cynicism, that safeguard, when a series of mishaps happened to him, such as being voted off SNL, or being kicked out of the Transcendental Meditation movement, he had no defenses. He couldn't cynically shrug it off. He'd feel the sting of rejection and couldn't release it. Did that sting internalize itself in the form of cancer cells, as Lynne suggests? Did they rebel and grow? Obviously a positive mental state has a lot to do with good health. Did this extremely healthy individual's own gene pool simply fail to cope with the "slings and arrows of outrageous fortune," even if he brought that "outrageous fortune" on himself? Did something in him just say, "It's time for Elvis to leave the building"? *Or,* did those rejections, mixed with his obsession about faking his death, reach such a crescendo that he finally acted upon it?

*   *   *

"I AM NOT A COMEDIAN!" He would yell it from the rooftops. Andy couldn't tell a joke to save his life. Wouldn't want to. He was however a bullshit artist, a master in the art of the humbug or "put-on," a prankster. Now most of the time, *laughter* accompanies a good prank. Maybe that's where the confusion came in. Usually at first people who are pranked are annoyed and don't laugh. But soon, if they have a sense of humor, they lighten up and go ahead and laugh with everyone else. Some don't. We've all experienced people in our lives like that. They're better to stay away from. Many of them don't have a sense of humor and after being pranked will say indignantly, "That wasn't funny." But Andy, on the other hand, always found life funny, if not downright hilarious. He had no use for people who didn't. In fact, if he stumbled upon one of these individuals, he took it upon himself to teach them a lesson by becoming even more obnoxious, sometimes even sadistically so. Eventually he would take on the entire entertainment industry, and he would either win or lose, depending on whether *you* had a sense of humor or not.

To some, Andy was a man-child. Michael Stipe of R.E.M., the band that wrote the homage to Kaufman in *Man on the Moon*, thought Andy was "a seven-year-old his entire life. I really feel like he was trying to lift us out of some morass of banality, of accepting everything for what it is rather than questioning it." Was Andy a wide-eyed innocent? Or was he a fearless and subversive outlaw, lampooning the mediocrity of the entertainment industry? To me, his writer for ten years, he was both. Did he ever sit down and openly discuss lampooning the mediocrity around us? No. He would never intellectualize about anything he did and hated when people tried. Andy could also be quite funny if he wanted to be and could construct a comedic scenario with the best of them, but then—a moment later—purposely bore the audience to death just to see how much they could take before they walked out. When asked whether he was concerned that this sort of behavior could cost him a mass audience, his reply was, "I don't perform for the masses. I perform for a small group who knows what I'm doing." I would even take it a step further and say Andy was performing for himself. Blissful self-indulgence. This attitude would keep his manager George Shapiro up at night. As for me, I was sharing the rocket ship with Evel Knievel. Director Judd Apatow said it best: "Where do you go if you're Bob Zmuda? After you write for Kaufman, how can you possibly write for somebody else?" You're right, Judd, you can't. So what do you do? Just keep writing for Kaufman! Dead or alive, it doesn't matter.

* * *

Alan Zweibel, one of the early and top writers from SNL, captured his first impression of Andy's genius:

> I heard about Andy Kaufman before I saw him. I remember they were talking about him and how he got fired from a club in Florida and they said why did he go there in the first place? Why would they understand him? And then I didn't really get what

that sentence meant. And then one night I was at the Improv and did see that Andy Kaufman was on. And I sat in the back of the room out of curiosity. So did the other comics. And I saw him do Mighty Mouse and thought I was going to go crazy. I saw him do the Foreign Man. Here was a guy that showed that you didn't need language, you didn't need English to elicit a response from an audience. I have never seen anybody and probably to this very day who could manipulate an audience any way he wanted to. When he would do Tony Clifton, he would get the audience to hate him. He would have the audience booing him. And then at the end he would have them cheering him. He would be able to take them any place he wanted them to go. And people started coming to the club to see this guy. At Rick Newman's Catch a Rising Star, Carl Reiner and Rob Reiner would come to see him. One night Woody Allen was there. On another, Dustin Hoffman. It was this phenomenon. People would come in and go, "Golly, I could never do a thing like this." I would never think that any-body could do a thing like this. I could never think that a thing like this should be done. But it is being done and look how great it is. It was so different than anyone's background orientation. I don't know how this happened. I was impressed. Besides his talent, there was a commitment there. He would meditate before every performance. There was a real commitment to what he did. He was unfailing. He just dug in. But I worried about him. I thought, "Where is he going to do this?" People write jokes, tell jokes, and take the check. Where was he going to go with this outside of the Improv and Catch a Rising Star? How was this guy going to make a living?

*   *   *

What drove Andy to do the things he did? As in most performers, I believe there was a level of narcissism at play. In Andy's case, throw in some sadomasochistic tendencies also. I say this because at times he truly enjoyed being rejected and hurt. Once Jeff Con-away, a cast member of *Taxi*, got drunk and started beating the hell out of him. He didn't even protect himself and took the beating, *à la* Gandhi. Emotionally and physically he was hurting, but Jeff believed, "He pushed me to do it and enjoyed it."

He wallowed in the pain. Another time, after being voted off SNL, he immediately went on *David Letterman,* making a routine out of the collapse of his career. I tell people, "Andy Kaufman died for our sins"—because I believe his psychological imperative in faking his death was martyrdom.

Yes, I believe that he faked his death. How can I think anything different? He talked to me about it endlessly for three years, and also to others. It would be his "greatest illusion," he said, and when he was gone, "people should be ashamed for they had the greatest performer in the world in their midst and blew it."

The consummate performer to the end, leaving them wanting MORE and sadistically punishing them by not giving it to them. "Father, forgive them, for they know not what they do." Music up: the theme from *King of Kings* plays. Roll credits. Is that where you are going to end it, Andy? Lifting Jesus's routine from an MGM biblical pic? But let's not forget the resurrection. Aren't you at least curious what a stir you'd create if you returned? That was the plan after all, wasn't it? Remember, you told Lynne, "Twenty or thirty years and I'll be back." Well, it's been thirty years! Mom and Pop are gone. If you wanted to walk on stage dressed in leather with a boy toy on a leash, be my guest. And don't worry about jail time. I'm sure you could easily pay back all those life insurance policies you ripped off in no time. We'd book you in the biggest venues around and charge top dollar. Who wouldn't pay to see the man who successfully faked his death? Andy Kaufman, the greatest entertainer of all time, returns. They always said you were twenty years ahead of your time. Well, perhaps now, thirty years later, the public has caught up with you. Give them one more chance. Your fans await you!

*   *   *

According to Andy, Janice Kaufman, his mother, admitted that it was her fault that Andy started to go to psychiatrists as early as age four. "I thought that children should always be happy and when Andy wasn't, I thought something was wrong." Andy said, "It's not that I was crazy, it's just that I was sad at times because the world was sad at times. When I would perform, it wasn't sad anymore."

I think Andy and I were kindred spirits in this regard. Both of our dads yelled a lot. I mean a *lot*. I remember going down into the basement of my home and performing to imaginary audiences just to get away from it. I would venture to say that many fledgling performers did the same. Performance was distraction from the harsh reality of life. When Kaufman and I met, we intrinsically knew this and from that moment on, the performances never stopped. It was 24/7. This nonstop act unleashed an overabundance of pranks, many times heaped on unwitting strangers, like it or not.

The fact that there were now two of us created a dynamic where one was constantly fueling the other. We were like the would-be murderers Hickock and Smith in Truman Capote's *In Cold Blood*. Alone, they wouldn't have done what they did to that unfortunate Clutter family. But together, they hog-tied and slaughtered them.

Kaufman and I together formed the same duo. We couldn't control ourselves or shut it down. We were hell-bent on "slaughtering" the status quo. I imagine we had a sense of youthful entitlement, but we weren't fascists about it. It was just fun. Fun was the key. Fun was the drug that fueled it all. Because if we were having fun, we wouldn't have to be sad. Fun … Funny … Humor … Comedy. You can see how the comedian label got wrongly applied. *Fun*. It's a word that can easily be taken for granted. People casually throw it around, as in, "We had a fun time." People who knew Andy will always use that word seriously in describing him, pointing out that fun really was his essence. Cindy Williams of *Laverne & Shirley* fame was a friend of Andy's. She elaborates:

As an actress who loved to act, I couldn't have met a better person than Andy, who acted every moment of his life. It was one big improv continuously. Such fun. The best fun I ever had in my life.

*   *   *

Lynne

Fun was everything with Andy. Breakfast was fun. We'd play the card game Crazy Eights for hours at breakfast because it was so much fun. Andy once challenged my brother Steve, who was a professional, world-famous card player, to a game of Crazy Eights. For fun. Sometimes we'd be driving in a car and pull up to a light. If there was a car next to us, Andy would start to strangle me and I would mouth "HELP!" to the car next to us, then when the light changed we'd speed off leaving them in shock. Just for the fun of it.

Another story: When I first got to San Francisco, I was living in an apartment with a roommate, Michael. Michael made a comment to me at some point that Andy used a lot of toilet paper. So Andy made it his mission that every night he would bring home a four-pack roll of toilet paper (always the same brand, of course) and put the pack on the back of the toilet. The pile grew higher and higher. Andy was waiting for Michael to say something, but he didn't. So Andy just kept adding packs until the pile reached the ceiling. Then he had me go in and ask Michael if he could get me down a pack of toilet paper because I couldn't reach it. That was the punch line.

*   *   *

Fun. It's the reason Andy chose me to be his writer. In fact, I was really more "Andy's actor" than "Andy's writer." We played and pranked constantly. Andy met his match with me. No matter when, no matter where, I "acted with Andy." It was always fun. That's why Andy became disheartened when his fun turned to work on *Taxi*. WORK IS NOT FUN! As the brilliant clinical psychologist Dr. Stan Martindale said, "Once they pay you for something you love doing, they kill it for you."

Andy realized early in life that kids got away with murder. Watch them in stores or supermarkets. They yell and cry, throw temper tantrums, and God forbid their mother physically reprimand them. Nowadays, a mom can run the risk of being thrown into jail. I am often asked, "Was that childlike nature Andy displayed a put-on?" The answer is "Yes … and no." You see, he too wanted to get away with murder, so he would turn it off and on whenever he chose, depending on the situation. At the high end of innocence you have Foreign Man; i.e., the lovable Latka character from *Taxi*. In Foreign Man's case, the innocence is amplified by the use of a foreign accent, making the character that much more vulnerable, as he tries to maneuver in a society that speaks a different language.

On Andy's first *Tonight Show* appearance with Johnny Carson, when he's invited to sit on the couch, Johnny is talking to him much like an adult to a six-year-old. In this case, he's dropped the foreign accent all together, but the Bambi eye movement, innocence, and shyness are all part of the act. Johnny doesn't know it at the time and believes it to be real. Besides, comedically it works for both pros. Later, on other Carson appearances, Andy turns it down quite a bit and starts acting more his age. This new dynamic throws Johnny, he doesn't know how to play Andy, and the laughter becomes less and less each time. Soon, Johnny realizes it's not working any more between him and Kaufman and doesn't invite him back, at least not when he's hosting. In retrospect, if Andy had maintained that childlike quality each time, he most likely would have been asked back countless times, and Johnny could have done his famous deadpan takes to the audience, much as he did with other childlike wackos like Charo and Tiny Tim.

But Kaufman didn't want to maintain that innocent character all the time. After all, there was a trunk load of alter egos just waiting in the wings, some of them bad guys who wanted to wrestle or the obnoxious lounge singer Tony Clifton who needed to come out. But innocence was in his arsenal of characters and could be summoned up whenever it was called for, even in everyday life, especially to pick up girls. That wide-eyed childishness just sucked them in. It was like a lost puppy they were gonna save. Once that puppy had got them in the sack, however, he would turn into a full-grown wolf—"Wanna wrastle?"

This man/child gimmick proved quite effective in business dealings also. Let the managers and agents bust their balls figuring out the best direction to take his career in. After all, they were getting a piece of the action. He'd just sit wrapped up in his innocent cocoon, spooning chocolate ice cream into his mouth like a child. He played the innocent to his manager, George Shapiro, through his entire career, and George would reciprocate by talking back to him in baby talk—much like his real dad did. Howard West, George's partner in Shapiro/West, knew it was an act and didn't buy into it, so Andy steered clear of Howard, choosing to deal with George instead.

With Lynne and me, he dropped the façade altogether. We wouldn't put up with it, nor would he want us to. Recently I was talking to Scott Thorson, who was Liberace's lover, played by Matt Damon in HBO's highly successful *Behind the Candelabra*. After watching Michael Douglas's portrayal of Liberace, I asked Scott if Liberace really talked like that. He said, "Hell, no. Only onstage. At home, he used his real voice." Same with Kaufman. At home, he used his real voice, at least around Lynne and me. Still, he'd cleverly work us sometimes with his hurt innocence when he really wanted something.

Like an artist with a palette of colors, Kaufman could mix and choose whatever character it would take to get what he wanted. I'm sure in the faking of his death, he had a whole other persona waiting in the wings, so he could live unrecognized. And I doubt very strongly that he would have flown off to live on some remote little island in the Caspian Sea. I think rather like Osama bin Laden, he would be hiding in plain sight, every day gloating in the satisfaction of his legendary disappearing act. Look around next time you go out. You just might spot him. Someone, someplace is probably standing next to him this very minute. By now he might be bald or have a beard and probably a good size gut to go along with it. Once he even told me he might have one of his legs amputated. This way no one would suspect him of being Andy Kaufman, who had two good legs.

This obsession with faking his death became just that—an obsession. No matter what time of day or night, if he had an idea or question about it and needed a sounding board, I was there, much to the chagrin of many a live-in girlfriend. Even though he never discussed how to fake his death with Lynne (after all, he was planning on fooling her also ... and did), the around-the-clock phone calls about anything and everything just kept coming incessantly.

*   *   *

Lynne

Oh, man, the phone thing. I hate talking on the phone and it's a testament to my love for Andy that I tolerated talking to him for hours at night when he or I were away from one another. He would talk endlessly because he knew it drove me crazy! I'd try to disengage and say I had to go to sleep and he'd say, "OK, good night ..." But then, just try to hang up! He'd say goodnight but not hang up, then you'd say "Are you still there?" "Yes, alright, good night" ... silence, silence, silence ... "Hello?" "OK, you hang up first." "No, you hang up first." "No, you hang up" ... for hours. Hours! But at the same time it was so much fun. Andy was like a little kid.

*   *   *

Ring …

B: Hi, Andy!

A: How did you know it's me?

B: It's three a.m. Who else would it be?

A: Sorry!

B: It's OK. What's up?

A: What's the name of that stuff that Juliet swallowed to make her appear dead?

B: I don't know. I think Shakespeare made up the whole story.

A: No, it was real! He just took it from some newspaper article he read.

B: Wait a second. Are you telling me Romeo and Juliet really happened?

A: Yes! We learned it in school. William Shakespeare wrote his play based on a real incident that actually occurred in Verona, Italy. You can actually visit Juliet's tomb. It's a big tourist attraction.

B: Is she in it?

A: I don't know. I never went. I guess she is.

B: Well, I'm sure if you researched it some, you could find out what it is. How long does it knock you out for?

A: I don't know. I remember once in science class, the teacher injected a live frog with the stuff or something like it.

B: What happened?

A: It died—or at least it looked dead. The next day it was hopping back around in its tank.

B: No shit!

A: Yeah, I saw it with my own eyes. If I can get ahold of some of that stuff, I'll swallow it, appear dead, and then come back when no one's looking.

B: How do you know when that's going to be? And how can you be sure no one's around?

A: Well, I would imagine after you die, like in a hospital bed, they take you down to the morgue. I can wake up there in the middle of the night. And if I already have the substitute body in the same morgue, I'll just switch toe tags. Then I'll put on a fake beard and clothes and simply walk out. Presto change-o! Look, I know it's not going to be that simple, Bob. Maybe I'll pay one of those Mexican guys who clean up there to help me. Most of those guys are illegal, anyway. They'd probably be happy to make a few extra bucks.

B: What if they wheel you down to the morgue and start performing an autopsy on you? Hell, they can kill you while you're still alive and not even know it.

A: Why would they need to perform an autopsy on me? They already would know what I died of.

B: And what is it you're going to die from?

A: I don't know yet. I'm still working on it. I'm in no rush. I won't do it until it's perfect. All right, talk to you tomorrow.

B: Great, Andy. Now I'm going to have nightmares about bodies in morgues.

A: You want me to send a hooker over? I got phone numbers. She could be there in an hour. It's on me. I had three working girls already this week.

B: Three? Why not just fuck groupies ...

A: They're more trouble than they're worth...You want a hooker?

B: No, save your money. You're going to need it. I don't think faking your death is going to be cheap.

A: But you do admit it's doable.

B: Of course it's doable. People get away with it every day.

A: Can you imagine how great this will be when I actually do it?

B: Well, just remember: If you get caught, they don't give out chocolate ice cream in jail. Speaking of jail, you better send me a piece of paper stating I had nothing to do with helping you.

CHAPTER 2

How Jim Carrey
Got the Job

Lynne

I slept on the couch in his room (Cedars-Sinai being the hospital to the stars, one could get away with anything there, doctors in the pocket of the famous). I rarely left his side. It was around 6 p.m. on May 16, 1984. Andy's condition hadn't changed and I hadn't slept for days. I lay down on the couch at the far end of the room and fell immediately asleep. The next thing I remember is hearing ALL the Kaufman family voices shouting, "Andy, hang on! Don't go!" I literally flew from the couch to his bedside. I can't recall my feet hitting the floor. When I got to Andy's bedside, he was surrounded by his family. There was no room for me at the head of the bed, so I stood and held one of Andy's feet while he died. (Hmmmm. Symbolic for how the Kaufmans treated me, eh?) Later, I was standing at the head of the bed, stroking and kissing his forehead; cold (holy shit, could that have been a body double?). I did see him (or whoever) take his last breath.

Then the nightmare of the Kaufmans invading my home. Andy and I had rented a house in Pacific Palisades after he found out about the cancer. Of course, HE rented the house, not me.

After Andy died, Stanley, his dad, "graciously" let me stay in the house for one month. After that, get out.

There they were in MY house. But they felt entitled because they were Andy's family; who the fuck was I? I had actually asked Michael, Andy's brother, a few days earlier if they would please move to a hotel because I needed solitude in my home. I remember that he just stared at me. He didn't respond. And I realize now it was because they didn't consider me of any consequence at all. It was THEIR house, not mine.

Lynne has had friction with the Kaufmans since then. This has escalated in the last few years to some serious threats of lawsuits. Andy would roll over in his grave … if he were in it.

*   *   *

Take your pick: either Andy Kaufman faked his death or he was a psychic. For it is an indisputable fact that he not only named the disease he would die of, but also the exact hospital he would die in of that disease, and he did it a full four years before he supposedly died.

It appears for all to see in black and white on page 124 of *The Tony Clifton Story*, a script that Andy and I wrote together for Universal Studios in 1980. I remember the day he rushed into our bungalow on the Universal lot quite worked up, nothing short of in a frenzy. "We've got to change the script, Bob. I just had a great idea." I said, "Fantastic. What is it?" He reached into his pocket and pulled out a piece of paper that he had scribbled on at 3:00 a.m. the night before and handed it to me. It read: "Tony Clifton dies of cancer at Cedars-Sinai hospital in Hollywood, California." We put it in the script. In 1984, "Andy Kaufman would die of cancer at Cedars-Sinai hospital," proof enough that he had decided four years earlier the exact disease he would use to fake his death and the hospital that he would stage it in. This fact has been recently verified by Universal Studios's script department, which has had the original script in its possession for the last thirty-five years. A statistician from the University of California—Berkeley ran an odds-predictability study listing all the possible ways one could die and a total of all the hospitals in the U.S. Statistically, the odds of someone's predicting what he would die from and the hospital he would die in are 780,000,000 to one. Basically an impossibility. That S.O.B. knew back in 1980 exactly what he would supposedly die from and where.

```
cob                          124

    127   INT. EDITING ROOM - KAUFMAN

          the film maker, is seated at a Steenbeck editing console.
          Frozen on the console screen is the footage of what we have
          just seen.  Kaufman turns straight to the camera and speaks

                              ANDY
                    My name is Andy Kaufman, maker of
                    the film you are now watching,
                    'The Tony Clifton Story.'  On
                    June 12, 1980, nine weeks into the
                    shooting...and just three scenes
                    away from the completion of this
                    film...Mr. Tony Clifton, at the
                    age of forty-five, died of cancer
                    at Cedar Sinai Hospital in
                    Hollywood, California.  On June 26,
                    1980, Universal Pictures unani-
                    mously decided to support the
                    countless actors, technicians and
                    various other production staff
                    members, in the completion of
                    'The Tony Clifton Story.'

          The camera moves in close

                              ANDY
                    In memory of Tony...and in all due
                    respect to him and his family, I
                    decided the last remaining scenes
                    would be completed, as written,
                    with myself playing the role of...
                    Mr. Tony Clifton.

                                        FADE OUT

          READER'S NOTE:  From now until the end of the film, Andy
          not only plays himself, but also Tony Clifton.  No attempt
          whatsoever has been made to make him look like Tony except
          for a moustache and hairpiece.  Even the tuxedo hangs
          loosely from his frame.  His portrayal of Tony is exagger-
          ated, to say the least.  The film continues where it just
          left off.

          FADE IN

    128   EXT. STAGE DOOR - TONY

          (played by Andy) running out of the door, into the rain.
          He hails a cab, jumps inside and speeds away.

    129   EXT. AIRPORT - HANGAR AREA - CAB
          pulls up in the rain.  Tony gets out and tosses a handful

                                                      CONTINUED
```

Actual page from *The Tony Clifton Story*, written in 1980, proof that Andy had decided four years before his supposed passing in 1984 what disease and hospital he would use to fake his death.

Equally remarkable is the last recording on the *Andy and His Grandmother* album (track 17), where the microcassette tape recorder catches Andy and me talking candidly. Out of nowhere, Andy comes up with the idea of faking his death for the first time. The recording ends with my saying, "Andy, you fake your death and nobody believes you, you'll go on forever ... immortal." Kaufman's reply is, "GREAT!"

When the Kaufman family heard of the release of the tapes, they tried everything in their power to stop it, sending threatening legal letters to both Lynne and Drag City, the company that released them. I couldn't help but wonder why they were so concerned. Was it Andy openly talking about faking his death? What were they trying to hide? I could only wonder if maybe they were in cahoots with him all along. Maybe Andy agreed with my thinking that it would be a cruel trick to make his mother believe he was dead when he wasn't and told her. Does track 17 reveal Andy's smoking gun? Did it have to be censored by the Kaufman family at all costs because it was a clear indication that he faked his death? What or who is in his crypt? His fans want to know. Just ninety minutes with a backhoe at the grave site and everyone can get a good night's sleep.

Working with Andy was like working with the great Houdini, and time and time again I'd see him go to incredible, painstaking lengths to pull off illusions. So why not this? Why not the greatest illusion of all time? And I wish I had a nickel for every time he called me, turning it around over and over in his mind on just how to get away with it. And those odds: 780,000,000 to one. How could he possibly have predicted the disease and hospital years before? And after all, wasn't it I who told him, "Andy, you even have to fool me." Had he even fooled Dr. Zmudee, as he called me? Maybe temporarily. After all, there was a body, wasn't there? There is a death certificate, isn't there? No, he did it. I know he did it. The brilliant bastard faked his own death, and he's going to return thirty years later, just like he said, and it will be the single most amazing event in the history of showbiz!

*   *   *

One day my phone rang—surprisingly, it was Danny DeVito on the other end. I'd met Danny a few years earlier on the set of *Taxi*, but that was nothing that would warrant a personal call. He was quite excited: "Bob, I have great news! Universal Studios is going to make a major motion picture about Andy's life, and I'm going to produce it through my company, Jersey Films. I'm even getting my old buddy, Milos Forman, two-time Academy Award winner, to direct it. And as Andy's writer and best friend, I want you involved in a big way. This film is going to be amazing." After my shock subsided, I congratulated Danny and told him how proud Andy would be of him. I then asked what he needed me to do. He said, "For now, nothing. I'll be contacting you in a week or so with more details. Till then, hold tight and don't tell anyone. I want everything signed, sealed, and delivered before we make an announcement." "I totally understand, Danny." Danny's last words to me were, "I'll call you back in no longer than two weeks." When I hung up the phone, I was ecstatic. Finally, Andy would get his due and, unashamedly, so would I. After all, ever since his "supposed" death, I had done everything within my power to keep his memory alive.

Weeks went by and every time the phone rang, I jumped, hoping it would be DeVito. Weeks turned to months. The call never came. I chalked it up to the deal's having collapsed, something that took place on a daily basis in Hollywood. I stopped anticipating that DeVito would call back. I figured he was probably bloodied by the studio. To save face, he just wasn't going to call back.

More time passed and I thought the whole matter was long dead. Then one day, my answering machine got a workout when call after call came in congratulating me on the fact that Universal was indeed making the film. Supposedly there was a huge write-up about it in *Daily Variety*. I ran to the nearest 7-Eleven and swooped up a half-dozen copies. I stood out in the street fighting the wind, trying to read the article. There it was in print, just as Danny said. Milos was going to direct, DeVito was going to produce with his partners Stacey Sher and Michael Shamberg, Larry Karaszewski and Scott Alexander would write the screenplay, George Shapiro and Howard West would executive produce. The film was to be called *Man on the Moon,* after the hit R.E.M. song about Andy. Everything and everyone was mentioned ... except ... except ... where the fuck's my name? ... except ... me!

I called a friend I knew from Universal when we had been developing *The Tony Clifton Story* before Kaufman's disappearing act. His name was Sean Daniel (*Dazed and Confused, Tombstone, The Mummy*). I told him my story. He concluded that I had "danced to the Hollywood two-step." I asked what the hell was that. He put it simply: "You've been cut out. Actually," he added, "You were never really in." "But DeVito called me," I said. "Obviously someone got to DeVito, Bob, and said we don't need Zmuda." "Is there anything I can do, Sean?" "Oh, yes," he said with great confidence. "Listen to me and do exactly what I say."

The letter Sean instructed me to send "to everyone" was polite yet firm. It sincerely congratulated all involved on how wonderful it was that Andy was finally being recognized. Of course, it also conveyed that since I, being his writer and all, was not involved, they did not have the right to portray a laundry list of material such as Carnegie Hall when we took the entire audience out in school buses for milk and cookies, him wrestling women, Tony Clifton, the Great Gatsby, the masked magician, the fight on *Letterman* with Jerry Lawler, and a slew of other pieces that I had also developed with Kaufman. In short, all they'd be left with was basically Andy playing the congas and singing to the Mighty Mouse record.

Soon my phone was ringing off the hook with apologies: "A mere oversight." In short order, I was made a co-executive producer on the film, allowed to choose whom I wanted to portray me, be downloaded by the writers Scott Alexander and Larry Karasze-wski, and most importantly, work closely with Jim Carrey, giving him insight into Kaufman and Kaufman's alter-ego, the notorious lounge lizard Tony Clifton. For all this, I was rewarded quite handsomely financially, along with a single-card producer credit in the film.

As for Lynne, she was in New York when she got the call that the film was being made. She was told that the writers, Scott and Larry, would like to interview her. She met with Scott and Larry at their office on the Sony lot. They told her that they were having trouble getting a fix on Andy. "A very key moment in the research for us," they said, "was interviewing Lynne. We said, 'We're looking for the real Andy Kaufman,' and she said, 'There is no real Andy Kaufman.'" Bingo! A light went on for them. It was a theme that was played out through the entire film. She had also given the studio tons of Andy's personal belongings to use in the film as well as advising the set designers on how his house looked, how he dressed, even what he ate.

When the film was going into production, Lynne had not heard from anyone about her being involved. (Sound familiar?) She had assumed, after meeting with Scott and Larry, and after giving the studio all of the memorabilia, that of course they would want her on board. After all, she was the love of his life—that should count for something. She called George Shapiro, who was executive producing the film with his partner Howard West, and set up a lunch meeting.

Lynne

He took me to Morton's steakhouse on La Cienega. (That was always one of the best perks about hanging with the Hollywood set. Great free meals and drinks.) I told George that I very much wanted to be involved with Man on the Moon. *He*

*said, "Doing what?" Well, that rather flabbergasted me into a
stuttered reply of, "Well, I'm not sure," and George said, "Send
me your resume and I'll forward it to Danny DeVito." I nearly
spit out my food. I wish now that I had, right in his face. In
those days, I was more intimidated by people than I am now,
and I just stared at him in silence. Later, Bob and I compared
notes and he told me that Stanley Kaufman didn't want either
of us involved. Why?*

Because Stanley (Andy's father) felt the story should be told through
his eyes, not ours, and he had already dictated to the writers the
scenes *he* wanted in the film. The scenes, besides of course co-
starring Stanley, also included a lot of revisionism. It's not that they
weren't true, but they were aimed at cleaning up Andy's image.
Stanley wanted to paint a more innocent, loving, and normal Andy,
a good Jewish boy who never missed Thanksgiving or Seders with
his family. Yes, Andy did drive a long distance to visit a girl who
was dying in the hospital. Yes, he did draw a crowd of people
around a woman who was collecting for a local charity and helped
her raise more money. Great, but not exactly the kind of scenes for
a motion picture about the world's greatest prankster. This wasn't
the Mother Teresa story, but the Andy Kaufman story. And Andy
himself had already laid the foundation for the script with his body
of work. But Stanley the overbearing patriarch and his family just
couldn't get that through their thick skulls. Or didn't want to. After
all, Stanley was acting like every needy actor who wanted to get as
much screen time as possible. Major studios do not make movies
of family albums. They make movies of remarkable people who
have done remarkable things.

The seldom-heard man behind the scenes, Howard West,
George Shapiro's partner in Shapiro/West, the management firm
that signed Andy, has what I feel is the most accurate assessment
of who Andy was from his no-nonsense, professional viewpoint:

I'd say to him, "What else are you going to do to wreck your career? You make things difficult, Andy! Dif … fi … cult!"

There was a self-destruct button in Andy. He was a daredevil, a high-wire act. I got this wire here. I can walk on it. Forty feet. Sixty feet. Eighty feet. One hundred feet. Maybe? That's a self-destruct mode. But it's also his talent. You can't separate it. Andy did what Andy had to do for Andy and did it well.

The real Andy you never knew or felt you knew. Nice, sweet conversationally, normal in his desires and wants, but I didn't see that much of that too often. Maybe others saw it with those he was closer to, like Lynne, and saw what we didn't see in their relationship. Mine was more career-oriented, with a few personal moments like talking about our hair loss, what can be done about it. That's a personal moment, when the veneer is gone, but I didn't have enough of those.

Once I met with Scott and Larry, I just dazzled them with the adventures Andy and I had together. Eventually they came right out and told Stanley, "We went with Zmuda's stories. They were better than yours." After hearing that, Stanley would hate me and the movie to the day he died.

With my newfound clout as one of the producers, I raised a ruckus and was able to get Lynne on the picture and paid. Still, first cuts are the deepest; the earlier snub by George and DeVito left its mark on us. After that, we never really trusted any of the executives who we felt tried to screw us, except for one, a producer by the name of Stacey Sher. Occasionally during the filming, DeVito would plead with me, "Bob, I had nothing to do with cutting you out of the deal. You gotta believe me!" Of course, he could never adequately explain why he never got back to me. Later, I would learn of similar transgressions by DeVito against others. I soon realized the cuddly Danny DeVito persona the public loves is in fact a power-driven mogul. Director Tim Burton, who is known to cast to type, scored a home run by casting DeVito as the Penguin in

Batman Returns. If you know DeVito the real guy, you know he is the Penguin when it comes to business, as diabolical as one could get.

DeVito wasn't always like that. When I first met him early on, when *Taxi* started, he was a regular Joe. It was funny—he and I had something in common. We both didn't have much money and drove beat-up jalopies. Both of our cars looked so bad that friends and business associates would tell us that we really shouldn't be driving these shit-cans onto the lot, as it was bad for our images. I remember having an exchange with Danny on this subject and he said something I'll never forget: "Bob, the day we're too embarrassed to drive those cars on this lot is the day we've sold out." Truer words were never spoken. Eventually both Danny and I got different cars. As Jonathan Nelson, an advertising executive, once said, "If history proves two things, one is that the avant-garde almost always gets assimilated, and two, young people get older." Yep, "times they were a changing." DeVito went for the Mercedes. My tastes were much more modest: a Land Rover, used.

As for Andy, he fought being co-opted with the best of them. The material possessions that fame and fortune brought he could do without, and did, except for one: "the pussy." Celebrity attracted pussy like nothing else and Andy couldn't get enough. After all, he had to make up for all those years when he was this unknown dork who was too shy even to talk to women. DeVito, on the other hand, seemed to be pretty grounded when it came to wife and family. If he had a mistress, her name was "Power." Andy's priorities were quite simple—TM first, and tied for second would be career and sex. As for the sex, he was insatiable. At first, groupies would do, but soon paid prostitutes became the order of the day.

Who would have predicted in those early days of *Taxi* that DeVito would go on to be a mogul and one of his passions would be to make a film about Kaufman? Why? Curiously, I feel I have an insight into that, and it came to light almost by accident one day when we were making the film. With Lynne's background in shooting documentaries, Universal needed an EPK (electronic press kit) for the film. So they threw a few extra bucks at Lynne to shoot it. It's simple enough to build. You shoot some B-roll here and there and a few short interviews with some of the principals involved. But here's where it gets interesting. One day, Lynne comes back to my trailer (as a co-producer I did get my own Winnebago) and she looked stunned. I said, "What's wrong?" She said, "Something weird just happened." I automatically said, "With Jim Carrey?" She said, "No, with Danny." She explained that while she was shooting him for the EPK, he started talking about how distraught he was when he attended Andy's funeral. I jumped in and said it the same time she did, "BUT HE WASN'T AT THE FUNERAL." "Exactly," she continued, "So why would he say that, when he wasn't there, nor were any other members of the *Taxi* cast except for Carol Kane?"

It all became crystal clear to me a few weeks later when it was time to shoot the funeral scene. And now things even got stranger, if not downright morbid. When shooting a film, especially a studio film, one of the advantages is you can make your movie on the lot. They have everything you need, as far as exteriors and interiors go. And for *Man on the Moon,* most of it was shot right on the Universal back lot. One of the exceptions was the funeral scene. For that, DeVito wanted to shoot off the lot at a real cemetery inside a real funeral chapel, which really didn't make any sense because we easily could have constructed a small chapel right on one of the sound stages. It was just an interior shot, anyway. So why go to the added expense of schlepping the entire cast, crew, and equipment out to the real location? I believe because this one scene to Danny was the most important scene in the movie and perhaps the real reason why he wanted to make the film in the first place—and that is he and the *Taxi* cast never went to Andy's funeral. And I believe that fact had been haunting Danny for all these years. But now he could change all that. He could right a wrong and rewrite history, for in his film not only he but also the entire cast of *Taxi* would be at Andy's funeral.

And that's just what happened the day we shot it. Everybody was there and to make it as real as possible, they spent $35,000 on a wax figure of Andy/Jim to lie in a coffin. Now they easily could have had Jim lie in the casket and grabbed the shot and saved thirty-five g's, but DeVito wanted that "dead body." He wanted himself and that cast of *Taxi* to be in a real chapel at a real cemetery. He wanted his cast to experience the funeral of Andy Kaufman they were never at but knew in their heart of hearts they should have attended. And now they were. I'll say it again: I believe that Danny DeVito made *Man on the Moon* specifically so he could shoot that scene and finally thaw out his frozen grief. Let me tell you, that day was probably the most gut-wrenching scene for all of us. Long after the cameras stopped rolling, Danny and his fellow cast members of *Taxi* sat perfectly still and wept openly, paying their last respects to Andy. And then the casket was slowly closed.

Months later, when filming had wrapped, the studio asked Jim if he wanted the wax figure of himself/Andy. He said no, it creeped him out too much. If you ever get a chance to watch *Man on the Moon*, look closely at that funeral scene, especially at the wax figure. Look how real it looks. Could a similarly realistic wax figure have been used at Andy's real funeral? Dr. Joe Troiani, a good friend of Andy's, attended Andy's funeral in '84. To this day, he will tell you that he believes the body at the Nassau funeral home in Great Neck, Long Island, was a wax dummy. Why? Because he touched it with his own hands. "I was alone with the body as it lay in the casket. Realizing that Andy and Bob were probably pulling off one of their elaborate pranks, I had no qualms about giving the corpse a few good shakes. No matter how hard I shook it, the head didn't budge one millimeter. It was as if it wasn't even attached to the torso. There is no doubt in my mind then or now that the whole thing was faked." Dr. Troiani himself will be in attendance for Andy's return to shake his hand for pulling off the longest prank in history.

Milos Forman, the director, is a star in his own right. Back when we shot *Moon,* he was sixty-six years old. He was handsome, with a captivatingly dramatic Czechoslovakian accent and two Academy Awards for *Amadeus* and *One Flew Over the Cuckoo's Nest* that he carried with him wherever he went (figuratively, not literally). A friend of Danny DeVito's, Milos had given DeVito his first film role in *Cuckoo's Nest,* starring Jack Nicholson. Remember Martini? A great performance by Danny. Now DeVito was the big dog at Universal with his Jersey Films company. DeVito's and Milos's paths crossed at some Hollywood shindig, and the subject of Andy Kaufman came up. Seeing that Milos had a pay-or-play deal at Universal for another project called *The Black Book,* which Universal wasn't too keen on doing but DeVito's company was hot on, the *Man on the Moon* project came together quicker than most. Milos had two young writers in his pocket named Scott Alexander and Larry Karaszewski. Besides writing *Ed Wood* for Tim Burton, they had just written *The People vs. Larry Flynt,* which Milos directed. They were immediately commissioned to start on the script and did extensive research on Kaufman. Once the script was completed and approved, casting began.

Here's where things got interesting. No sooner did the word get out that a biopic was being made by Universal Studios about Andy's life, directed by the legendary Milos Forman, than a slew of major motion-picture stars began to clamor to get the role. Tom Hanks, Sean Penn, Jim Carrey, Gary Oldman, Ed Norton, Nicolas Cage, Kevin Spacey … the list went on and on. We were all stunned. This was quite problematic for Milos. You see, Milos is what they call a gun-for-hire director. He shoots a movie every eight years. Between movies, he and his much-younger and gorgeous wife, Martina, enjoy the good life of fine wine and dinners with well-known personalities from all walks of life. One night Milos the raconteur might dine with Elton John and the next night with Henry Kissinger. All these stars wanting to play Kaufman put Milos in a precarious situation. What if the next movie he made depended on one of these stars to get financing? If Milos had rejected him for *Man on the Moon,* he wasn't very likely to think kindly of Milos next time.

So he came up with a clever plan. He would get the word out that if anyone wanted to play Kaufman, he'd have to make an audition tape, thinking many of them would say, "Screw that," and simply withdraw, not having to get rejected and cloud a relationship down the road with the Czech director. His plan paid off and many walked away. Secretly, Milos wanted his buddy Ed Norton to play the role. Ed had played the lawyer to Woody Harrelson in Milos's previous outing, *The People vs. Larry Flynt.* Norton was Lynne's first choice too. When she saw *Flynt,* the moment Ed Norton walked onscreen she leaned over to her friend Wave and said, "If they ever make a movie about Andy, that's who should play him." Danny DeVito wanted Jim Carrey, whose box-office appeal would be sure to open the film big. I personally wanted Nicolas Cage to play Andy. There was something about Cage that reminded me of my best friend. Besides, at the time, Cage had a list of stellar performances such as *Leaving Las Vegas.* Somehow Cage got my number, and he and I spoke quite often. I assured him that he had my vote. As Andy's writer, best friend, and now co-executive producer on the film, I knew my voice as to who should play Andy was a significant one, and I wanted Cage. Period. Nothing and no one was going to change my opinion.

It wasn't long before I got the phone call I dreaded most. It was from Jim Carrey. I knew Jim previously, but only briefly, when he was still an up-and-comer and shot a vignette for me a few years prior for the Comic Relief charity that I am the president and founder of. Now Carrey was a major star, the highest-paid actor in Hollywood—$20 million a pic. Jim's own story of success could be a movie itself. He's Canadian, never finished high school. His family was poor, his dad a sax player whose career never really took off, but a great guy. His mom and sister filled out the rest of the clan. From the time he was very young, they all knew Jim had a special talent. He could impersonate anyone. Not just celebrities like Elvis and Clint Eastwood, but the typical guy off the street. It was sort of uncanny how he did it. He has this physicality to his impressions that are spot on. You can sit with him in a restaurant and point to any one of the patrons and say to Jim, "Do him," and within seconds his whole physical being morphs into that person. Frankly, I've never seen anything like it. When young people come up to me today and ask how to get into show business, especially stand-up, I always tell them the Jim Carrey story. How he worked at Mitzi Shore's The Comedy Store on Sunset in Hollywood for eight years—two shows a night—for FREE! It was only when he befriended the Wayans Brothers, who themselves were just starting out and they got a show on Fox called *In Living Color* with an all-black cast, that things happened for him. They needed a "token white" and Jim was their choice. Remember Fire Marshall Bill? Every time he was in a sketch, he killed.

Soon, he caught the eye of a young director named Tom Shadyac. Shadyac was looking for the lead of a film he was about to direct, *Ace Ventura: Pet Detective.* They risked everything on Jim's scene-stealing, over-the-top, broad physical comedy, which no one was doing at the time and didn't want to. The gamble paid off and *Ace Ventura* was a monster hit, with half of America quoting Jim's lines from the movie, such as, "Allllll rightteeee then!" He followed it up with other films (such as *Dumb and Dumber, Liar Liar, The Truman Show*, and my favorite, *The Cable Guy*, produced by Judd Apatow) and now he had his heart set on playing Kaufman.

Jim was still a struggling comic at the Store when Andy and I would come in and test new material on the audiences. Comics would sit in the back of the room, mouth agape in awe of Kaufman's antics that left audiences either loving him or hating him. Either way made no difference to Andy. He was operating from a whole other gearbox. Carrey would later say, "The comics would watch Kaufman and say, 'Just make a statue of the guy already. He's a god!'" The chance to play his comedy hero would be a dream come true. Somewhat spookily, added to that, he had the same birthday as Andy, January 17. He was going to play Kaufman come hell or high water, and now he was calling me.

B: Hello?

J: Hi, Bob, it's Jim Carrey.

B: Jim. How are you?

J: Fantastic. You probably can guess why I'm calling you. I made the audition tape and before I embarrass myself and show it to Milos, I wondered if you could come and take a look at it.

B: I'd be happy to. [*I wasn't happy at all about wanting to see it.*] When?

J: How about right now?

B: NOW!?!

J: Yeah, if that's OK.

B: Yeah, sure. What's your address?

On my way out to Brentwood, I kept saying to myself, "No matter how good it is, don't say anything that he could take to the bank"— i.e., don't say, "That's great." Say something like, "Very interesting." Remember, I didn't want him. I wanted Nic Cage for the role.

Jim's house in Brentwood is fab-u-lous! Although modest by movie-star standards, Jim's digs made my humble home in Burbank look like a hovel. Jim greeted me at the front door. We walked through his house out into a back yard that had one of the best swimming pools I've ever seen, designed out of natural rock. It had a waterfall pool on a top level that also served as a Jacuzzi that cascaded into the main pool. Off the pool was a pool house that housed a bar and various arcade games.

He led me into another building that was his own movie theater. Jim's costumes from all his films (*Ace Ventura, The Mask,* The Riddler from *Batman Forever, The Cable Guy*) lined the walls, sealed behind Plexiglas. The room was designed to impress and it did. Besides hiring a projectionist just for me, he had a fully stocked concession stand with everything your tummy could desire: candy bars, popcorn, soda, ice cream, etc. Jim said, "Bob, excuse me, but I have about ten minutes of phone calls to finish up. Then I'll be back with my audition tape. Help yourself."

He pointed to the candy counter and left. As soon as he was out of sight, I greedily started filling my pockets with SweeTarts, M&Ms, licorice, Nestlé Crunch, Butterfingers—you name it. I figured I might as well stock up—I'd never hear from Jim Carrey after today. I was going with Nic Cage.

With pockets bulging with goodies, I nestled into my cozy theater chair, my buttered popcorn and Coke overflowing onto the thick-carpeted floor, waiting for Jim to return with the "audition tape." Jim had playing on the large screen old clips of Andy on *Taxi* and SNL. I stared at the real Andy Kaufman and thought how surreal this whole experience was and wondered if Andy was going to forget his thirty-year deadline, cut it short, and show up at the premiere. For all I knew, perhaps Andy was already sequestered away somewhere on Jim's palatial estate.

Ten minutes later, as promised, Jim walked back in, carrying a small brown paper bag. He stood next to me and said, "And now for my audition tape." Next, he reached inside the bag, fishing around for something. A puzzled look came upon his face, as if it was lost. And then he violently tore the bag open and started laughing like a mad man. It was empty. His laughter grew, to me, more sinister and in the dark theater, with only him and me, I got creeped out. I thought, "Who's to say a movie star couldn't also be a serial killer?" Then in a grand gesture, he pointed to the movie screen. The old clip was of Andy playing the congas on SNL, and he said, "So, what do you think of my audition tape?" At first, I hadn't a clue what he meant. And then it hit me: Oh my God, that wasn't an old clip of Andy on SNL. It was Jim. I had been watching the clip from SNL for five minutes and just assumed it was Andy. Instead, it was Jim, and he nailed it.

Get this: He had his buddy, director Judd Apatow, shoot the scene. They rented a studio and matched up the SNL set to a T. Jim had even taken conga lessons four times a week for three weeks just to learn how to play them for the "audition tape." He hadn't even been given the role yet. That's Jim Carrey. When he wants something, he goes for it full steam. My jaw dropped. I couldn't believe he had bamboozled me and in such a Kaufmanesque style. I must admit my eyes moistened as I watched my best friend come alive through the talent of Jim Carrey. I told him right then and there, "As far as I'm concerned, you got the role." A broad smile appeared on his face. He knew he had it anyway. I would find out later Jim's like that. He knows what he wants, goes for it, and gets it every time. He's the second-most driven person I've ever encountered in my life, the first being Andy, of course.

I didn't hang around for long now that he had sold me on his performance. I refilled my pockets with goodies and left. He was ready for stage two. As soon as I drove off the property, he must have had four deliverymen on motorcycles with audition tapes in hand peel out and scatter in all directions:

1. To Milos, staying at the Beverly Hills Hotel
2. To Ron Meyer and Stacey Snider, executives at Universal Studios
3. To Michael Shamberg and Stacey Sher at Jersey Films
4. To Danny DeVito's house in Malibu

By the time I got back to my shithole in Burbank, there were already three messages on my machine from irritated executives who lambasted me for telling Jim he had the role. He had obviously called them. Ten minutes later (after they too had viewed the tape), they all called back and apologized: "Of course he has the role." He *was* Andy Kaufman. Fuck Nic Cage. I never called him back. I was as bad as DeVito was about returning phone calls.

Now here's the punch of all punches: A year later, when the film was shot, edited, and presented, I was at the opening-night premiere. There was a grand party afterwards, and as I was consuming my alcoholic beverage of choice at the bar, I felt a tap on my shoulder. Lo and behold, it was Nicolas Cage. Before I had a chance to tense up—after all, I'd stopped returning his calls—he immediately put me at ease and said, "Bob, it's OK. I couldn't have done what Jim did. He was fucking great." We shared more than a few cocktails, and as it turned out he and Jim had been close friends for years. Then I asked him, "Nic, why didn't you make that audition tape?" "Oh yes, the audition tape. Well, the reason I didn't make the audition tape was because my good buddy, Jim Carrey, told me, 'Guys in our position shouldn't make audition tapes.'" Then he broke into uproarious laughter. I just shook my head and smiled: Jim Carrey. I rest my case.

Now that Jim was cast, Universal left it to me to choose who should play me, although I did consider their suggestions. On the top of the list were Philip Seymour Hoffman and Paul Giamatti.

One Saturday night, I received this bizarre phone call from Milos at 3:00 a.m., telling me he had found the perfect person to play me: GARTH BROOKS! I was in shock. "Garth Brooks, the country western singer? Milos, he isn't even an actor." Milos informed me that Garth had hosted SNL that evening. Milos watched it and said the guy was terrific. Come Monday, I got a tape of the show and sure enough, Garth held his own with the Not Ready For Prime Time Players. And "Bob Zmuda played by Garth Brooks" sounded crazy enough to work. If not, at least I might get laid in Oklahoma.

Messages were sent back and forth between Garth's people and Milos. Did Garth understand that besides playing me, he also had to play Tony Clifton, Andy Kaufman's alter ego, just as I had done for Andy over the years? Brooks understood. In fact, he wanted the role so badly, I was told he canceled one of his sold-out concerts on a Saturday to fly to LA and have dinner with Milos. Much to Milos's surprise, he walked into the restaurant dressed like and doing a spot-on impression of Tony Clifton. Milos loved it and wanted to give him the role, but at the last minute, Brooks's agency had a change of heart and decided against it. Brooks, not to let the experience of playing Tony fall by the wayside without some payday, a year later summoned up his own alter ego by the name of "Chris Gaines" and released an album in that name, giving himself a goatee and a whole other look. The album didn't do so well, but I did get a kick when a reviewer from *Rolling Stone* said, "It looks like Garth lifted the alter-ego idea from Andy Kaufman's Tony Clifton." Little did the reviewer know that he'd hit it right on the head, even though he never knew about Garth's doing Clifton for Milos. For a while, I considered Philip Seymour Hoffman. I went to the video store and rented *Boogie Nights*. I was in for a real shocker when in the film, Philip Seymour Hoffman tried to kiss Mark Wahlberg. I thought to myself, "Jesus Christ. I don't want some gay guy playing me," and nixed Hoffman immediately. Years later, I was in the American Airlines lounge at Heathrow Airport and I spotted Philip making out with one of the hottest young chicks I'd ever seen. They were really going at it, and I thought to myself what a dummy I was. He wasn't gay. What he was was just one hell of an actor. I was quite saddened years later when I heard that Philip had died of a heroin overdose.

Eventually, with Lynne's help, I chose Paul Giamatti, a great guy just like myself. Besides, like they say, Brad Pitt wasn't available.

When I hired Paul to play me, I made him promise to do one thing. "What's that?" he asked. I said, "Play me more intelligent than I really am." He laughed and said, "Oh … that won't be a problem."

I drove Paul nuts on the set, overanalyzing every little motivation and gesture. One day, Milos yelled at me in front of everybody, "ZMUDA! Leave Zmuda alone!"

Meanwhile, Lynne was spending time with Courtney Love, who played her. Lynne told me, "I felt so sorry for her about all the conspiracy theories that she had killed Kurt Cobain. Shit, I felt horrible being treated badly by the Kaufmans, and here she had people saying she had killed her husband. Horrible."

Once Lynne and I realized that Jim was going to approach the role of Kaufman in a "method acting," Kaufmanesque kind of way—i.e., he would become Andy or Tony Clifton for the entire shoot, never breaking character—we realized this had to be captured on tape. So Lynne, Universal Studios, Jim's production company (Pit Bull), and I agreed that we would all partner up and shoot a documentary of Jim's journey into "channeling Kaufman."

Since Jim the star wanted it, Lynne as cameraman and I had free rein to shoot anywhere and at anytime, much to the discomfort of Milos and the rest of the crew. Seldom did the camera leave Lynne's shoulder, and after a while, she became a fly on the wall and almost disappeared, offering us the opportunity to document some pretty bizarre happenings. Jim arrived at the studio every day in character, stayed in character all day, and went home in character. In fact, Milos Forman didn't meet Jim until principal photography was over eighty days later.

Jim had researched Andy, who himself would always stay in character. In fact, when Andy would become Tony, he did so for three or four days. Bill Knoedelseder, a reporter for the *Los Angeles Times,* who spent much time interviewing Andy and Tony, believed that "Tony Clifton was a *controlled* multi-personality disorder; i.e., Andy suffered from multi-personality disorder. And since he was in show business, always looking to present the absurd, it was natural that he would present Tony to his audience." Andy kept a pink Cadillac convertible in his garage and drove it only when he was Clifton. Andy also was a strict vegetarian who didn't drink or smoke. Tony was just the opposite, a chain smoker who was always slugging from a bottle of Jack Daniel's. He'd eat steaks rare and run around town with hookers on his arm. Jim's Clifton mirrored Kaufman's in this regard … except for the hookers part. When you're Jim Carrey, you don't need to pay for it.

When we were shooting at Universal, Jim insisted that Lynne and I have lunch with him on the front porch of Alfred Hitchcock's *Psycho* house. Jim would dress as Norman Bates's mother, in granny dress and grey wig. Occasionally, when an unsuspecting Universal tram of tourists would drive by, Jim would jump out of his chair, pick up a real axe, and run after the tram, smashing into it, actually denting the hell out of the vehicle. The unsuspecting tourists thought it was just some minimum-wage actor Universal had hired to give them a scare. They were much more interested in the guy in the Frankenstein suit. Little did they know this was superstar Jim Carrey. Axe-wielding granny tore through those Universal tourist trams like Godzilla tore through Tokyo. I thought this was pretty rad, reminiscent of the golden days of Hollywood when stars could literally get away with murder and the powerful studios would mop it up. Carrey had balls as big as Kaufman's. Lynne and I were really beginning to like this guy. He was a daredevil like Andy.

If Jim was the 800-pound gorilla, Courtney Love was the original bad girl of punk. Nobody could see her in the demure role of Lynne—nobody except Milos, who insisted on casting her. After all, Milos had just worked with her on his last film, *The People vs. Larry Flynt,* where she played the drugged-out wife, Althea Leasure Flynt (to Woody Harrelson's Larry Flynt), who eventually ODs. She was spectacular in the role, and even received a Golden Globe nomination. But the word on the street was she was basically playing herself. In fact, the film company for *Flynt* wouldn't insure her, believing she was going to show up on drugs, or, worse, not show up at all. Milos had to put up his own paycheck as collateral.

So the first day she showed up on the *Man on the Moon* set, nobody knew what to expect—especially Jim! It was lunchtime. We were out on location, the whole cast and crew gathered under a large tent. Someone had hired a four-piece mariachi band to go along with that afternoon's Mexican cuisine. Lynne and I were sitting at a table with Jim when Courtney entered. It looked like she was just about to step into the shower. She wore no makeup whatsoever, but was still a pretty girl. She wore a white robe that was loosely tied. Immediately she began to dance and spin to the beat of the mariachis, every spin loosening the robe more and more, giving revealing peeks of a killer body. She had nothing on underneath and frankly didn't care. More than a few of the crew put down their tacos and adjusted their chairs to get a better view of the action. She did not disappoint. She seductively worked the room. Someone yelled out, "Courtney Love, ladies and gentlemen!" and the room broke into spontaneous applause.

She eventually made her way over to Jim and held out her hand to join her. Jim, without missing a beat, suavely got up from his chair, grabbed her hand and pulled her to him. Next he flung her out where she gracefully spun a triplet, only to be once again retrieved by Jim. They both were flawless, and the now-audience responded with applause. Damn! Courtney knew how to make an entrance.

By now, the robe had totally opened itself up. Courtney's breasts, though small, stood out perky and proud for all to see. Jim, not to be outdone by his leading lady, ripped off his shirt, much to the delight of the ladies. Courtney reciprocated by dancing ever more provocatively. Obviously this was becoming a test of wills as to who could be more outlandish. Jim wouldn't be outdone. Just as the music was drawing to a close, he undid his belt, threw it into the crowd, unhooked his pants, unzipped his zipper in rhythm to the music, and—just as the backbeat hit—pulled down his pants. The place went wild. Jim won! As he should. After all, if Courtney was going to play Lynne to Jim's Andy, she had to learn to step aside and let her man shine, which she did. I realized right there and then, just like Jim did, she'd make a great Lynne. She could be subservient. Courtney Love knew how to act.

Things really got out of hand the day we shot the recreation of Clifton's being thrown off the Paramount Pictures lot. Talk about a surreal experience. Here they had brought back the entire cast of *Taxi* (minus Tony Danza) and we recreated that legendary day. Jim, as Clifton, drove onto the lot drunk and started to ram into the side of the soundstage that housed the *Taxi* set. Mortar and bricks were flying all over the place. Anyone else would have been shot. But security was held back while Carrey, deep in character, kept throwing the car in reverse and smashing, smashing, smashing the structure, exorcising Kaufman's spirit. That afternoon, Clifton on the set broke down in real tears between takes. DeVito and Carol Kane joined in. They openly wept for Andy. This was hallowed ground and the real Kaufman's ghost permeated the reconstructed *Taxi* set and could be strongly felt—all brilliantly captured on tape by Lynne. At the end of the day, Clifton was carried into the limo dead drunk and totally spent. This was no longer a movie being shot; this was a full-fledged psychodrama, and we have the tapes to prove it.

Many months later, when Jim's good friend, director Rob Reiner, saw our documentary and a rough-cut screening of *Man on the Moon* back to back, he told Jim that Universal should shelve the motion picture and release the documentary instead, as it, according to Reiner, "was a truer representation of Kaufman's art." For years, Lynne and I have been trying to convince Jim to release it. It's the most intimate and truthful work of Jim's career. His coming up the ranks as a nightclub impressionist before he was an actor taught him early on to work from the outside in. Our documentary afforded him the opportunity to work from the inside out. For that reason alone he may be oversensitive about its being seen by others.

"Dailies" is the term used for the previous day's shooting. It's processed overnight and gives the various departments of camera, sound, lights, costume, hair, sets, etc., a chance to see how everything looks blown up on the big screen. Since only twenty-four hours have gone by, it's a safety device used just in case something is amiss so it can be reshot before the set is taken down. On our first day of dailies, much to everyone's surprise, none other than Tony Clifton (played by Jim Carrey) struts in bigger than life. You should have seen Milos's face. Very seldom does the star of the film show up for dailies. Obviously it's the star second-guessing the director's work even if that director, in this case, has two Academy Awards on his mantel. So Clifton plops his ass down right in front of Milos and yells, "Lights out. Roll 'em." Clifton's persona was so over-the-top authoritative the poor projectionist just did as he was told. The scene they were looking at was one of Andy's, not Tony's. Clifton quickly barked, "NOT GOOD! TOO MUCH! HE'S PUSHING!!" Then Clifton got up, turned to Milos and scolded him, "YOU'VE GOT TO WATCH THAT GUY." And then Tony and his entourage (us) left. Basically it was Jim's way of telling Milos, "Watch my impression of Andy. Make sure I'm not overdoing it"—which he was and caught it. It wasn't a lecture the legendary Milos was used to hearing. But that's Jim's work ethic. That's why he's numero uno. His motto is, "I don't care who you are or how many Oscars you may have, it's my career and I've been this successful in it so far because I scrutinize everything." Someday I'd love to see Jim direct. He could do it. He can pretty much do everything. Milos hates stars. He'd rather work with unknowns.

Also in the screening room that day was Michael Hausman, who line-produces all of Milos's films. He's appalled at Clifton's behavior. How dare he bark orders at the maestro Milos, let alone bring a documentary crew in on the dailies? Lynne with her camera would be a constant thorn in Hausman's side for the entire filming of *Man on the Moon*. But there was nothing he could do.

What Jim said was law. Hausman had to bite the bullet on a daily basis. Never before in the history of a major motion picture was a documentary camera (Lynne's) given the free range to be everywhere and anywhere she wanted to go. Lynne never overstepped her position, and everybody in the cast and crew soon learned to love her, as she truly is one of the sweetest people you'll ever meet. After a time, she blended into the woodwork and caught a behind-the-scenes look at Hollywood that only insiders see. A truly extraordinary achievement.

*   *   *

Everybody went crazy. I mean everybody. Biopics bring out the worst in everyone. *Man on the Moon* was no exception. Every family member, past girlfriend, college buddy, or fan who might have met Andy for five minutes felt the movie should be about Andy and them. The film's writers, Scott Alexander and Larry Karaszewksi, interviewed everybody. We already knew that the biggest role besides Jim's would go to Andy's manager, George Shapiro, played by Danny DeVito. DeVito was executive producer on the film and his Jersey Films was the production company, so obviously George Shapiro's role was going to be well taken care of, as it should have been. George was a big part of Andy's career and nobody handled trying to explain Andy's bizarre methodology better to the suits than George did.

Now George and I had a love/hate relationship. Originally, when Andy brought me on as his writer, George welcomed me with open arms. After all, Andy was a lot to deal with, as most talent is. Talent needs constant hand-holding, and the personal manager's job is to do just that. When I came on the scene, at first George was relieved. Now he had someone to field the constant phone calls other than himself. Over the years, when my power base grew with Andy and I had his ear, George didn't like it so much. Looking back over Andy's career, I'd say my one great regret was that George and I didn't communicate enough with each other, if at all.

It wasn't long into the process when DeVito turned on his own director, Milos. Milos didn't like the script that Larry and Scott had written, even though it was Milos who had brought Larry and Scott in. DeVito was clever when Milos started throwing his weight around and wanted to do a rewrite himself. Danny quickly bonded with Larry and Scott who, like all writers, didn't want one word on *their* script touched, and so he was able to quickly turn them against their old pal Milos. DeVito even sealed the deal by giving Scott and Larry another job writing another script for him and the promise of even letting them direct it, which they did, which also got them out of town for the whole *Man on the Moon* shoot, "coincidentally." Another smart maneuver on DeVito's part, making sure Milos and his writers couldn't join forces again.

So now DeVito had the writers in his camp. Milos was furious and ran off and wrote his own script over a weekend. I never read it, but Danny, Scott, Larry, and Stacey said they didn't like it. When he handed it in Monday morning, it was in longhand, hard to read, with numerous misspellings. Its central theme, as much as they could decipher, was that people intrinsically know if they're going to die and therefore their subconscious seeks to get as much living in as possible before the clock runs out and that's why Andy created Clifton, according to Milos's version. Interesting concept.

So here we were a few weeks away from shooting and Milos wanted to throw the whole script out and start from scratch. Well, this went over like a lead balloon. DeVito told Milos, "No fucking way." He must do the script they gave him. Michael Hausman's take was, "How dare they question the great and infallible Milos Forman?" DeVito now seized the opportunity and offered to direct the picture himself, which is what he wanted all along. Here's where I came in to exact my revenge against Danny. I by now had Jim Carrey's ear and told him of DeVito's plot to dump Milos. Jim wouldn't hear of it. After all, he signed on to the film to work with two-time Academy writer-director Milos Forman, not Danny DeVito. Milos wasn't going anywhere, thanks to me. Besides, he wasn't about to lose a multimillion-dollar payday. So we started our film with everyone basically hating and distrusting everyone else. Poor Jim. He was flying solo and needed to channel Andy more than ever.

*   *   *

To add to the clusterfuck, Stanley Kaufman still harbored resentment that the movie wasn't about him and Andy. All the rest of us, including George, should be secondary characters. Stanley, who had an ego comparable to Danny's, Milos's, and Jim Carrey's combined, as family patriarch now poisoned the rest of his offspring, Michael and Carol, to hate the script also. Dumb, dumb, dumb. Here you have a major studio spending a shitload of money making a film on a not-very-known performer to begin with, and the family's attacking the film. How fucking stupid can you get? Not only were they looking a gift horse in the mouth, they wanted to send it off to slaughter before it even had a chance to run around the track.

Milos, now pissed off about having to direct a script he wasn't crazy about, bit the bullet and did his best.

After production wrapped, I had a final dinner alone with Milos, where he confided in me that he had never before had his producer turn on him and try to take the film away. He said it was the most miserable experience of his career. He was so distraught over it he managed to get no more than three to four hours of sleep a night while shooting. It was a damned shame. Milos deserved better.

If it wasn't for producer Stacey Sher, who showed up every day on the set buzzing with enthusiasm and love for the project, it would have been a total disaster.

Well, if they, like all the others, couldn't get their shit together to make a film, at least Jim, Lynne, and I would. That film wasn't

Man on the Moon, but the little documentary we were shooting that we named, appropriately, *Andy Lives.*

*   *   *

Ring …

B: Hello.

A: It's Andy.

B: What's up?

A: I figured it out.

B: Figured what out?

A: I die at sea! NO BODY. It makes it a whole lot easier. There's a boating accident and I fall overboard. It's night. Everybody thinks I've gone under, but I'm a strong swimmer. So I'll swim away a good distance and then you can pick me up in a powerboat.

B: I already told you I can't help you with this one. What if they give me a lie-detector test?

A: Why would they do that?

B: Because they'll suspect you faked your death.

A: Why would they suspect that?

B: Because you're running all around town blabbing about it!

A: No, I'm not.

B: Yes, you are. John Moffitt told me you went over to his place and made him and Jack Burns swear on a Bible that they wouldn't tell anybody about your plans to fake your death.

A: Who told you that?

B: John Moffitt!

A: Damn it, he wasn't supposed to tell anyone. He swore on the Bible.

B: He's a Jew. He could give a shit about the Bible.

A: I thought if you swore on a Bible, you had to keep that promise.

B: Andy, you've been watching too many *Perry Masons*. Since you've told some people, they're not going to believe this "lost at sea" con. You need a body. And you need to quit telling people your plan.

A: Bob, don't worry. It'll all work out in the long run.

CHAPTER 3

Sneaking into the Playboy Mansion

Like a top athlete, Jim had Lynne and me as trainers in all things Kaufman. Put-ons were the order of the day, much to the chagrin of Milos's henchman, Michael Hausman. None though was more elaborate than the one we played on Mr. Playboy himself, Hugh Hefner.

It all started when Jim received an invitation to attend an event at the Playboy Mansion. It was called "A Midsummer's Night Dream"—a pajama party at Hef's pad for the rich and famous. But this was not just any pajama party. This was the pajama party of all pajama parties. Playboy had pulled out all the stops, as it was the first party Hef had given in years, because for the last nine, he had been married to Kimberley Conrad, the mother of two of his children. When Kimberley asked for a divorce, Hef was devastated. Once again, at age seventy-two, he found himself a bachelor. The Playboy organization, on the other hand, loved it. For too long, Hef was a dutiful husband and father. All those sex romps that he was known for in the early years before marriage was what Playboy was all about. Now once again a free man, he removed the kids' toys from the house and replaced them with new toys of a vibrating nature. "A Midsummer's Night Dream" would be Hef's coming-out party, and no expense was spared. It was the hottest ticket in town, and since Jim was the hottest star in Hollywood, he was at the top of Hef's to-get list. There was only one problem: Jim didn't want to go. He thought the whole thing silly. To him the Playboy philosophy had played itself out back in the '60s and '70s. If Jim wanted to meet hot girls, all he had to do was leave his house and show up at any number of trendy Hollywood nightspots. Within minutes, he'd have any girl of his choosing going home with him. Why did he need to dress up in a pair of silk pajamas and satin slippers and suck on a pipe not even filled with ganja?

I, on the other hand, a Chicago boy who grew up in the city where Hef started the magazine and the first Playboy Club and where Playboy for years had its corporate office, thought an invite to his first big party in ten years was, "Hell, yeah!" Damn, if Jim didn't want to use the invite, I surely would.

By now, Lynne and I realized that Jim was a real recluse and very seldom left his digs except to be driven to the studio to work. We had encouraged him to get out. Besides, Lynne and I needed a break from Jim, as we didn't want to get burned out. He said he'd consider it. But as the date grew closer, he just couldn't muster the enthusiasm to go. Then one day, he had a brilliant idea, a very Kaufmanesque idea. Jim Carrey wouldn't attend, but Tony Clifton would. He told his assistant, Linda Fields, to get Hugh Hefner on the phone. He had a plan.

Jim had never met Hefner before, and Hef was excited to take the call. Jim explained that he was working on *Man on the Moon*, that he was totally absorbed in a character named Tony Clifton, and that he'd be happy to attend "A Midsummer's Night Dream" but only under two conditions: 1) He'd come not as Jim Carrey but as Tony Clifton, and 2) Hef couldn't tell anyone that Tony was Jim. Jim said if people knew that Tony was Jim, it would defeat the whole purpose of being in character and in that case he'd rather not come. Hef happily agreed to both conditions, eager to get Jim there in any form.

As Jim sat in a chair in his living room, Ve Neill, the makeup person from the film, applied the Clifton prosthetics to his face. Jim was in the chair over an hour. I was in the kitchen having a snack, while Lynne was testing her video and sound equipment. Jim had cleared it with Hef to bring along a videographer, as we were making our documentary. This in itself was apparently earth-shattering, as Hef never allowed cameras in his lair. Jim was nearly finished when I phoned my home to check messages. There was one from Bill Zehme. Zehme was a friend of mine from Chicago, a good writer who had written a book himself about Kaufman called *Lost in the Fun House*. He had also written a book about Hefner called *Hef's Little Black Book*. He was letting me know that he had heard the rumor (obviously from Hef) that Jim was going to be there dressed up as Clifton. He was calling to know if it was true. When I told Jim about the message, he just about hit the roof. "That FUCKING Hugh Hefner. I told him not to tell anybody. Well, FUCK him! He blew it. I'm not going." He leapt out of the chair and quickly started ripping the Clifton prosthetics from his face. He was pissed. We all were. What a bummer.

Fifteen minutes later, Jim perked up. "Wait a second ... I've got it—two can play this game. Tony is going to go tonight, except it won't be me. Zmuda, it's going to be you!" "What?" I said. "NO WAY!" I hadn't done Clifton in years and told Jim so. Jim pleaded, "Come on, Bob. You can do it. It'll be good for you to get back in the old fellow's skin. Come on, Lynne, tell him he's got to do it." Lynne encouraged me also. The next thing I knew, I was sitting in the makeup chair. Ninety minutes later, I was Tony Clifton.

Here was the plan: I, as Tony, along with Lynne, would jump into the limo and go to the Mansion. Hefner would believe that under the makeup I was Jim. But, exactly at 11:00 p.m., Jim Carrey would show up as himself. If everything worked out, Hugh Hefner would be pranked, and it would all be caught on tape for our doc. The only caveat that Jim insisted on was that he would not reveal that he knew Lynne and Tony and would act just as mystified as to our presence as Hef would be—i.e., once caught, Lynne and Tony would be on their own, and whatever trouble they were in, Jim wasn't going to bail them out.

Jim had ordered up the biggest stretch limo he could find for Clifton. Heads turned as it barreled down Sunset Boulevard toward the Playboy Mansion, which was lit up like a Christmas tree for the occasion. Limos were backed up waiting at the guard gate where credentials were checked to ensure only the *crème de la crème* were let in. Immediately, Clifton—tossing $20 to his chauffeur—had him start laying on his horn, signaling the limos before him to hurry up. Certainly not the right protocol for such an esteemed lot. When that didn't work, Clifton lowered his window, stuck his head out, and started to yell obscenities.

"Hurry up, assholes, I don't have all day. Let's move it, I don't want all that hot pussy to get cold." The security guard at the gate looked dumbfounded and appalled.

When Clifton's limo finally arrived at his gate, Clifton was beside himself. *"What the fuck, man? Next time you hear me toot, you let me right in. I wait for no one, let alone these Hollywood wannabes."* The guard, unimpressed and already hating Clifton, looked at his clipboard and said, "Name?" Clifton snapped back, *"Name! Are you shittin' me? Everyone knows me. I'm a household name, for Christ's sake!"* The guard repeated more firmly, "NAME!" Clifton, becoming more irate, spat back, *"The name's written on the bottom of my shoe, and soon it's going to be up your motherfuckin' ass—which by the looks of you you'll probably enjoy. That reminds me, how do you get a gay guy to fuck a girl? Put shit in her pussy!"*

The guard was not amused, turned his head slightly, and spoke into a small microphone mounted on his lapel, "Code 14. Troublemaker. 10-4." Clifton said, *"Troublemaker? The only trouble, fuck face, is the trouble you're going to be in if you don't let me in immediately. I'll sue you, your children, and your children's children."*

Lynne interceded, realizing that if this kept up they weren't going to get in. "His name is Tony Clifton." Clifton reprimanded her, *"Don't tell him shit."* The guard scanned his list up and down. "No name like that on it." Clifton screamed, *"I DON'T NEED MY NAME ON ANY LIST. I'M AN INTERNATIONAL SINGING SEN-SATION, AND I WANT THE RESPECT DUE ME. YOU BETTER LET ME IN OR I'LL REPORT YOU TO THE BETTER BUSINESS BUREAU."* The guard turned back to his lapel mike, "There's some asshole here named Clifton. He's not on the list." While they were checking on the other end, Clifton yelled, *"I'll give you thirty seconds and then I'm turning around and going to Larry Flynt's party. His girls are much younger than Hef's old broads in their twenties and are will-ing to flash their buttholes."* The guard was stunned when the word came back over the speaker to let Clifton in. "OK, you're cleared." Clifton continued, *"Damn right I'm in, and you're out. I'll have your job. How old are you?"* The guard wouldn't answer. *"I said, 'How old are you?'"* Just to move Clifton along, he answered, "Thirty-eight." Clifton fired back, *"Thirty-eight! And this is all you've made of your life? Pathetic. Truly pathetic."* With that, Clifton's driver drove on to the house. You could hear the guard back on his microphone saying, "You got a real piece of shit coming your way. Ten-four."

When Clifton got out of the car, a small band of Hef's security surrounded him. But by now word had reached the party inside that Clifton (wink-wink, Jim) was outside starting trouble. Everyone in the house rushed out to catch the fun. I remember Jon Lovitz was one of the first to arrive. Carrey as Clifton was a dream come true for Lovitz. This was history in the making.

Clifton demanded that *"Hefner come out of his den of iniquity to personally greet me or I'm going to leave."* A few nervous minutes went by while Clifton slugged from a bottle of Jack Daniel's he was holding. Meanwhile, Lynne was out of the limo diligently shooting away. Soon the master of the house made an appearance with the two luscious blonde twins he was banging at the time.

Hefner was ecstatic that Jim ... I ... I mean *Clifton* ... was there. He improvised with Tony. "Did I invite you?" Clifton reached into his pocket and pulled out his invitation, which was nothing more than a crumpled-up, Jack Daniel's-stained Xerox of the original invite. Hefner looked at it front and back. "It's a Xerox! And it's sticky!" The gathered crowd laughed. Clifton fired back, *"That's right. So it's a Xerox. And I had to relieve myself on the way here!"* The crowd loved Tony's inappropriate honesty. Hef turned to his assembled guests and in a loud voice said, "Should we let him in?" A roar of approval went up. With that, Hef put his arm around Tony's shoulder and said, "Come on in."

The gate had been breached. Let the festivities begin. Inside, there were Playboy Bunnies in the skimpiest of lingerie, with tits strategically overflowing their halters. Hef knew each of their names and prided himself on introducing them to his special guest. Some of the girls would occasionally screw up and say, "Hi, Jim" instead of "Hi, Tony." Hef would shoot them a scornful look. Hef made the rounds, his arm still slung around Clifton's shoulder, not letting go until he had introduced his "prize possession" to the most powerful in the room. Only then did he release him to the bundle of Bunnies, who swarmed around him like bees. Clifton was in heaven. One of the girls whispered in his ear, "I'm your biggest fan." Clifton whispered back, *"So meet me in the grotto in a half hour. You like anal?"* The girl's face at first looked shocked, but quickly recovered. After all, this wasn't just any schmuck who wanted up her poop shoot, but Jim Carrey. Twenty million dollars per picture. The Bunnies lived at the Mansion just hoping a celeb of his magnitude would take them away from it all.

An hour later, Clifton was getting down on the dance floor. All eyes were on him as he twisted, dipped, and even moonwalked. The dancing caused him to sweat quite profusely. And I worried that Clifton's prosthetics would start coming loose.

Tony waved Lynne over and frantically whispered in her ear, *"Call Jim. Tell him to hold off for another hour. I need to knock off one of the Bunnies in the grotto before he gets here. This may just be the greatest day of my life."* Lynne called Jim, who was sitting in his limo drinking a milkshake waiting for us to give him the OK to come up. She got him to hold off for a while, but on the second call he said he was on his way no matter what. The plan was that Jim was going to show up and Hefner would be stunned, not knowing who Clifton was, thinking it had been Jim. Gotcha, Hef! If Jim was going to show up soon, Clifton had to move into overdrive. He quickly grabbed one of the hottest Bunnies there, took her into a nearby bathroom, and closed the door. Within minutes, she was all over him. No less than ten minutes later, he gave her a facial. When he finally unlocked the bathroom door, three other Bunnies admonished the girl for "keeping Tony for herself." Clifton was just about ready to go back into the bathroom with the other three when one of Hef's security people came up to him. "Mr. Clifton, Mr. Hefner's been looking for you. Follow me." Clifton excused himself to the girls, *"Don't go anywhere. There's plenty of me to go around, if you catch my drift,"* accentuating *"drift"* by grabbing his dick through his pants. They giggled. As the guard escorted Tony to Hefner, I (Bob) couldn't help thinking that I must have died and gone to heaven. What it must be like to be Jim Carrey every day!

When Hef spotted Tony, he ran up and once again put that trusting arm around his prize. "Tony," he said, "I want you to meet a very good friend of mine." He walked over to a table and he tapped a very distinguished older gentleman with perfectly coiffed white hair. "Tony Clifton, meet Tony Curtis." Curtis was everything an aging movie idol should be. He wore an ascot and had on his arm a six-foot-two-inch long-legged blonde bombshell—his recent wife. Curtis was quite impressed meeting Jim … I mean Tony. So was his wife, who gave Clifton a look that if he wanted some, it was his for the taking. Curtis knew that look and gave his own look to Tony signaling that it was OK with him and perhaps they could share.

By now, time had run out, and with Hef's arm still snugly around Clifton's shoulder, enter super-duper star Jim Carrey. The room went silent. You could hear a pin drop. Wait a second, if that was Jim, who was this impostor that Hef had his arm around? It all happened so fast, but felt like slow motion. It seemed that everyone had spotted Jim but Hef. When he did, it was one of the greatest double takes known to man. Remember, Hef's arm is around Clifton. He turns his head and spots Carrey. It doesn't register at first and he turns back to Clifton. Then it hits him like a ton of bricks. His head snaps back to Jim, who waves at him. Hef snaps his head back to Clifton and quickly throws his arm off of this charlatan's shoulder. Hef stands there frozen in time, trying to make sense of it all. Soon, his face begins to turn bright red, while his twitching jugular vein becomes more and more pronounced. He looked as if he was going to have a heart attack. (I was worried for him, for he had a heart attack not more than a year before.) He was furious and grabbed Tony's wrist hard, *real* hard. Through clenched teeth, he whispered in Clifton's ear angrily, "I don't know who you are or how you got in here, but if all these people weren't around, I'd have my goons break every fucking bone in your body."

By now, his security had sensed something was terribly wrong. Within seconds, they were all over Clifton and Lynne. Hef whispered something in a security guard's ear and they were quickly escorted not too gently out of the Mansion. Hef composed himself and went to greet the real Jim Carrey. Remember, the deal with Jim was that under no circumstances was he going to come to Clifton's and Lynne's rescue. Lynne and I were on our own and were unceremoniously hustled out through the garden behind a shed. I was scared that I was going to get quite a beating, especially when I saw the guard I had insulted at the front gate on the way in. Quickly walking over, the guard snarled, "I knew you were an asshole." He reached for Lynne's camera. She frantically tried to pull an old switcheroo on the tapes but wasn't fast enough. We were then quickly taken to the back gate, next to the trash cans, and thrown out. It took a while for us to realize we weren't killed, and then we broke into uproarious laughter. Lynne kept repeating, "Holy shit! Holy shit!"

Meanwhile, back inside, Hef is explaining to Jim what just took place. Jim's playing dumb. Hef explains that he got a call from Jim saying he was coming as Clifton. Jim stops him right there and says, "Mr. Hefner, I never called you." Hef shakes his head in disbelief and says, more to himself than to Jim, "These people were good. Real good!"

When Lynne and I returned to Jim's house that evening, I removed Clifton's prosthetic pieces from my face. I was ecstatic. Had we really pulled it off? We stayed there late, waiting for Jim to return so we could compare notes. A couple of hours later he did. Jim was overjoyed that we put one over on Hef. Hef told him how he had introduced Clifton to the royalty of Hollywood, thinking it was Jim. I'm sure the Bunny with Clifton's facial was scrubbing her face raw with a washrag at this point, realizing she was facialed by a fraud. Jim, Lynne, and I celebrated by uncorking a bottle of Jim's finest champagne. We toasted Andy Kaufman and, most important, Jim got to see firsthand how a Kaufman prank could be pulled off and especially the lesson of how dangerous it sometimes could be. Lynne and I could have gotten the shit kicked out of us, and Hef's people would have been justified, as we were party crashers, and obnoxious ones to boot. To this day, I've got to salute Hefner and his crew for keeping their cool. Lynne and I knew from working with Andy in the past that possible physical harm came with the territory. If you weren't willing to bleed for your art, then why do it?

I woke up the next morning feeling both happy and rotten. It hit me that it was only a matter of time for Hef to put two and two together. Bill Zehme, who had called me originally telling me how Jim was coming as Clifton, would have compared notes with Hef. They would have realized that Jim was lying to him and that Bob Zmuda had fucked with him. Not good. Hef had attended a few

Comic Reliefs in the past and I didn't want to be on his shit list. Remember, I was still a boy from Chicago and he was one of my heroes. Who wants Hugh Hefner to hate him? I quickly called Jim and told him I was coming over, as we had to talk.

When I got to Jim's, I explained my reasoning for coming clean with Hef. Jim didn't want to go down as a liar with Hef. Besides, I reminded Jim that Hef's security had confiscated Lynne's tape. It was great stuff. We had to get our hands on it before Hef had it destroyed.

We jumped into Jim's car and drove back to the Mansion unannounced. Seeing that it was Jim, security readily let him through the gate. Hefner was inside. It was Sunday afternoon, and every Sunday afternoon Hef held screenings of classic films for his immediate friends and Bunnies. When Jim and I walked in, Hef was in the middle of telling those gathered about the Clifton ruse the night before. He said, "I'll tell you, I've never seen anything like it in all my years. Nobody ever gets through my crack security team. NOBODY. But they did. I don't know who those people were, but it was real Mission Impossible-like stuff."

Hef couldn't believe his luck having Jim make an appearance two days in a row. "Jim, what are you doing here?" "It's about last night, Hef. I wanted to come clean. I was in on it. Like I said, I'm right in the middle of shooting the Andy Kaufman film and this fellow next to me is Bob Zmuda. He was Andy's writer. And last night he was Tony Clifton, a role he and Andy shared." Hef sized me up, trying to comprehend what Jim was saying. Jim continued, "Andy, as you know, pulled pranks. So in the spirit of Andy, we decided to pull one on you. Please forgive us." "Forgive you?" Hef said. "It was brilliant. Bob, you've got some balls. I have one security guy who wanted to clean Clifton's clock out." Then Hef walked over to his desk, picked up a videocassette, said, "I think this belongs to you," and handed it back to Jim.

We spent the rest of the afternoon at the Playboy Mansion. I ran into the girl who Clifton had given the facial to. God, she was even more beautiful in the clear light of day. But then, as Tony would say, *"My jism is known to get rid of wrinkles."* Later on, she was sitting in the parlor, rubbing Hef's neck. Our eyes met, and she smiled. I looked down, somewhat embarrassed. After all, I wasn't Tony, just plain old Bob. Where's Clifton when you need him?

*　　*　　*

Doing Clifton is like doing drugs. The more you do him, the more you want to do him, and the darker he can become on every outing if you don't watch it, as Robert Louis Stevenson found in *Dr. Jekyll and Mr. Hyde.* At first, Hyde is a lot of fun, pushing the boundaries of acceptable social behavior. But soon he becomes more brazen in his sinister behavior until he totally engulfs Dr. Jekyll. Kaufman and I would discuss this metamorphosis at great length: Was Clifton destroying Andy's career? When Jim Carrey signed on to do the role, I forewarned him of these same dangers. Could Clifton injure Jim's career as well?

We would soon find out, for probably one of the most controversial episodes in Andy Kaufman's career was when he, as Tony Clifton, was bodily thrown off the Paramount lot by security. Therefore, when the day came for Jim Carrey to recreate that scene, he too needed to put himself into the mindset of career suicide. So how does a handsome, $20 million per pic superstar get himself fired? Easy. He gets a billionaire who owns the whole damn studio to actually throw him out FOR REAL!!!

In all the months that Lynne and I had been working with him, we had never seen him put himself in such a dangerous professional position. I saw real terror in Jim's eyes that day. Had he finally gone too far in his quest to play Clifton? Was he now doing things that could actually jeopardize his own reputation? The sick bastard in me could only hope!

That day Jim, already in makeup as Clifton, drove onto the Paramount lot. He was unusually cordial to the guards at the gate.

This time he had to be. After all, he needed to get onto the lot to begin with in order to terrorize it later. Once in, he made a beeline straight for the commissary. Lynne and I followed closely, she with the documentary camera hidden low by her side. We entered the cafeteria. It was around lunchtime. The maitre d' sat us among the other diners, made up of production personnel and studio executives. It was pretty much a chi-chi crowd with a hefty-priced lunch menu to match, thus keeping the studio's day laborers and working stiffs out.

Immediately Clifton's voice shattered the tranquility. He saw two gentlemen nearby who were being served their dessert—chocolate cake. Clifton demanded that their cakes be put aside for him, as there may be not enough left. At first, the men tried to laugh and shrug it off, but Clifton only turned up both the volume and his obnoxiousness.

It wasn't long before he got the attention of another gentleman who was sitting further away, but was now himself swept up in Clifton's bravado. It was Sumner Redstone, the billionaire owner of Paramount Pictures. He was not amused by Clifton. Remember, nobody knows this is Jim Carrey. Even if Redstone knew it was Jim, I don't think it would have made much of a difference anyway. Hollywood has a class system all its own. Mere millionaires and stars like Jim to Redstone were a dime a dozen, meaning nothing. Soon one of his henchmen came up to Clifton and asked him to "hold it down." I could see Jim was scared, but at the same time struggling to be true to all things Andy. He apologized by saying he suffered from Tourette's syndrome and couldn't control what came out of his mouth. The henchman walked away … Clifton apologizing? This was unheard of!

And then I watched closely to see Clifton's next move. This was the moment of truth—would Jim cave or not? After all, one of the most powerful men in town had just sent his goon over and told Clifton to behave himself! Seconds seemed like hours—would Jim fold? And then Clifton leapt to his feet and started strutting around the room singing, "HIGH HOPES!!!" loudly while occasionally telling diners, "DON'T WORRY—YOU'RE ALL GOING TO MAKE IT!" Soon security was back and demanding that he leave. I looked over at Redstone and he was not amused. We were escorted out. Clifton was now primed to shoot the scene of him being thrown off the Paramount lot.

The next day Jim told DeVito what had happened. DeVito found it hysterically funny and decided to give Redstone, whom he knew, a call to tell him Clifton was in fact Jim Carrey. DeVito was taken aback that Redstone still didn't find the humor in it all. Jim took a bullet for the team. Believe it or not, diligent documentarian Lynne captured the whole thing on tape by keeping the camera hidden. One day hopefully Jim will release the doc and you'll get to see for yourselves just how brave he was. Just like Andy.

For years I've been haunted by those words Clifton kept repeating to those at the Paramount commissary: "DON'T WORRY. YOU'RE ALL GOING TO MAKE IT!" What did Clifton mean by it? What did Jim mean by it? I now believe it was a rare insight into Jim Carrey himself. As Clifton (a man with Tourette's), Jim let it slip. I believe he was telling us all sarcastically through Clifton that fame and fortune is an illusion. It's not all what it's cracked up to be. It will not save you. He knew it would not save him.

Even though Lynne's and my main job was to provide Jim with as much insight into Andy as we could, and in Lynne's case also assist Courtney Love with the nuances of Lynne and Andy's relationship, still from time to time we found ourselves on the set when a scene would be filmed that we knew never took place in real life. Usually in such cases, we'd simply hide out at the food truck or use the opportunity to return phone calls. When one of our characters was in one of these scenes, we couldn't help but be anxious about what dialogue the writers were putting into our mouths. Nine times out of ten they got it right, but occasionally when they got it wrong, it was excruciating for us and almost impossible for us not to speak up.

In my case, there was one scene in particular where George Shapiro (DeVito) was scolding Andy (Jim) and me (Paul Giamatti) as if we were two little kids. This scene was driving me crazy mainly because it never happened in real life. George may or may not have scolded Andy when they were alone together, but George never would have scolded me. Our relationship wasn't like that. George and I were equals and always respectful of each other.

So when they were rehearsing the scene, Giamatti could see me wincing off camera. During a break in the action, he came up to me to ask what was wrong. I told him point-blank, "It never would've come down like this." He asked me what I thought we should do about it. I told him since it was one of DeVito's big scenes, I didn't want to make waves.

When they went back to shooting the scene and George started his scolding again, Giamatti improvised and said, "George, don't be such an asshole!" I almost fell out of my chair! DeVito hated it. After all, who likes to be called an asshole? Later, Lynne told me she saw Danny go up to Milos right afterward to complain about it and suggest using a different take. So I was quite surprised when I saw the final film and Milos had left it in. I can't help but think that Milos got a little revenge.

One day while filming, the true test of the Courtney/Jim chemistry would be played out in an intimate scene between Lynne and Andy. The set was cleared with only technicians essential to the shoot remaining. Jim (Andy) and Courtney (Lynne) are in bed together. Milos softly whispered, "Action!" In the scene, Andy is distraught after being kicked out of the TM movement. It's Lynne's job to make him feel better, but there's a big problem: Courtney's not feeling it. She said, "Milos, can we cut?" The camera stopped rolling. Not good. She then asked for Lynne. The whole production came to a screeching halt until Lynne could be located. Once she arrived, Courtney pulled her aside and said, "I needed to be near you to pick up your calming energy. I went to the MTV Music Awards last night, and I'm still in my 'corporate rock star' persona.

It's not working for the scene. I need to get into my Laurel Canyon hippie mode." She then held Lynne tightly, drawing in her energy. Afterwards she hopped back into bed with Jim and nailed the scene in the next take. Courtney's a pro. She knew just what she needed—"the Lynne fix"—got it, and delivered the goods. It's a shame she doesn't choose to go out for more roles. She is one hell of an actress.

*   *   *

Probably the most dangerous, yet most successful, Kaufmanesque antic that was pulled off in the filming of *Moon* was Jim Carrey's neck injury. It was art imitating life, or vice versa, when Jim suffered the injury while filming a scene with the same professional wrestler who once put Kaufman in a neck brace, Jerry "the King" Lawler. What really made it strange is that they were recreating the exact scene when Lawler (on April 5, 1982) also sent the real Andy Kaufman to the hospital.

Tensions ran high on the set when Lawler first showed up, hoping to meet Jim Carrey. Instead, he met a totally deep-in-character Jim, a bitter rival. Jim started in where Andy had left off years ago when he was still alive and had suffered a serious neck injury when Lawler was wrestling him and gave him the notorious "pile driver," one of the most illegal moves in wrestling, which has left many over the years paralyzed. Jim would seek Andy's revenge.

The first day on the set, Jim attached a paper sign with tape to Jerry's back without his knowing it. It read, "Hulk Hogan wannabe." All day, Jerry walked around the set with cast and crew laughing at him and him not knowing why, until the very end of the day, when Andy/Jim pointed it out. Jerry's face turned red and he was truly embarrassed. Andy would further get his goat by mockingly talking to him in an unflattering hillbilly accent: "You're in my neck of the woods this time, Lawler, and I own this town." On another day, Andy would taunt Lawler by tossing him a bar of soap and saying, just as Andy had done years prior, "This is a product we've been using up North for some time now. Perhaps you can introduce it to the South. It's called 'soap.' Spell it with me. S-O-A-P—soap." Another time, he'd toss him a roll of toilet paper, saying, "This is another product we've been using up North. It's called TOILET PAPER. If you folks down South used this, there wouldn't be this stench in the air."

This kind of taunting went on day after day as long as Jerry was on the set. It was taking its toll on Lawler, who was not a method actor like Jim and subsequently told the line producer, Michael Hausman, that this behavior was uncalled for and might lead to a real physicality if Andy didn't stop. Hausman contacted Jim's management with his concerns that someone could get hurt. Once Andy heard of the complaint, instead of stopping, he only increased the taunts. More than a few times, Lawler would go after him, but thanks to Hausman, who had posted more security to keep the two apart, blood had never spilled (so far). Yet unfortunately, there was one more scene to be shot with Lawler and Andy in two days, and in this one, because it was a wide shot, Universal security couldn't be in the frame. Tensions ran high.

Everyone was concerned, so much so that line producer Michael Hausman pulled me aside and asked if he could speak off the record. He had never liked the idea that we were filming a doc during the making of his and Milos's film, but had learned to bite the bullet and live with it. But he dropped all pretense and began to talk to me man to man.

He truly was concerned for Jim's safety. Jerry Lawler's manager, Larry Burton, had warned him numerous times that Jim's methodology of taunting Jerry was causing Jerry to come unhinged and if it didn't stop, he could not guarantee what Jerry might do. Hausman told me he and Milos totally understood the acting approach Jim was taking but felt that ... I finished his thought, "A Southern boy like Jerry doesn't appreciate a sophisticated New York City

Lee Strasberg method acting technique." He said, "Your words, not mine." If I could get Jim to lay off a little, he'd appreciate it.

That night, I couldn't sleep. I really didn't want to interrupt Jim's process and yet at the same time, I didn't want to see him hurt and the picture shut down. Over lunch the next day, I decided to talk to him about it. He saw that I was truly concerned for his safety and agreed to stop taunting Jerry, so much so that he thought it would be a great idea to bury the hatchet and invite Jerry and Larry to his house that evening for dinner. Great!

He sent me as his emissary to speak to Jerry and Larry about it. They accepted the invite. It was for 9:00 p.m. at Jim's, and Carrey was going to have his personal chef pull out all the stops and create a truly spectacular feast for the four of us. Jerry asked what they should wear. I told him casual would be fine.

I got to Jim's house about 8:30. His chef was in the kitchen cooking up a storm. The main course would be beef Wellington (one of my favorites). I started lifting lids, seeing what other culinary delicacies awaited us. I was just about to lift one more when the chef stopped me and, with a sly smile on his face, said, "Don't look. That one's a surprise!"

I left for the dining room where Jim was arranging the table himself, laying out his finest silver and imported French place settings. I noticed that the settings (only two) were at the end of the table where Jim and I were to sit. Jim had already uncorked one of his finest bottles of wine to breathe and two crystal glasses awaited, but nothing at the other end of the table where Jerry and Larry were to sit.

Jim had a devilish look on his face. I said, "What are you up to?"—fearing the worst. Here was Jim's plan: Once his guests arrived, he would sit them at the other end of the table. The chef would enter, pour wine for Jim and me and then begin to serve us, all the time leaving Jerry and Larry at the other end with nothing. Only after we were served would the chef walk over to Jerry and toss two paper plates in front of them. Then he would leave and reenter with that mysterious pot he wouldn't let me see before. It contained hot dogs and beans, which he would unceremoniously dump on their plates. Next he would plop down two cans of beer, while Jim would say, "I thought this might make you feel more at home!" I placed my hands over my eyes and shook my head, saying, "Oh, no!"

I thought to myself, "Jerry's going to kill him." Soon it was 9:00, then 9:20—9:45—10:00. Still no Jerry and Larry. Jim was beginning to fume. The perfectly prepared medium-rare beef Wellington was beginning to turn well-done. Jim had me call Larry. He answered. It sounded like he was in a bar. I said, "Jesus, where are you guys? Jim's growing impatient!" Larry said, "What do you mean?" "What do you mean, what do I mean? You were supposed to be here over an hour ago." "We were?" Larry acted dumb, as if he didn't know about it. Obviously they were jerking Jim off. I hung up and had to break the bad news to Jim that he'd been stood up. Jim was at first hurt and then furious! Jerry had decided to play hardball and had no intention of showing up. Jim sent the chef home. The beef Wellington—overcooked and dried out—went to the dogs, and Jim started to drink and plot his next move.

Soon, he jumped up, ran to the phone and began to dial. "Hello, is this Le Dome? This is Jim Carrey. I know you're closing in a few minutes, but could you possibly stay open? I'll be there in a half hour with a party of eight. You will? Great! See you soon." Next Jim had me call Larry back and tell him that Jim had just made a reservation for all of us at Le Dome, and Jim was calling four of the top call girls in Hollywood to join us. The entire evening would be on Jim!

I'm thinking to myself, "To hell with the beef Wellington, these four dishes Jim was going to call up would easily make up for it." Next I waited for Jim to call "the lay-deees"! Instead, he walked into the kitchen and came out with the pot of hot dogs and beans and asked if I wanted any. I said, "Hell, no, I'll eat at Le Dome." He said, "We're not going to LE DOME." I said, "What about the call girls?" He said, "There are no call girls. I made it up. I'm gonna give Jerry a taste of his own medicine." He had me call Le Dome thirty minutes later. Jerry and Larry had arrived and were waiting. The maitre d' asked how soon Jim would arrive. After all, he had kept his entire staff over just for him. Jim had me say, "We're on our way." Another forty-five minutes later, Jim himself called back, and he told the maitre d' he'd changed his mind and wasn't coming. They should tell the two gentlemen (Jerry and Larry) to leave. The maitre d' wasn't too happy about it until Jim told him that he would compensate him and his whole staff well for staying open, which I found out later he did—very well, I might add. Usually I would have found the whole night's episode amusing, but I couldn't help shake the ominous thought that kept clouding my mind ... "If Jerry wasn't thinking of hurting Jim before, after all this, he'll kill him!"

The next day the stage was set for a major confrontation—Jim and Jerry wouldn't even look at each other until they started filming. I told Lynne no matter what happened to keep shooting, knowing she would anyway.

The scene was a much-detailed recreation of Kaufman's famous wrestling match with Lawler in '82 at the Memphis Coliseum, when Kaufman and Lawler faced off with each other alone in that "squared circle," the wrestling ring. To make matters worse, Andy/Jim wanted Lawler to actually give him the "pile driver" for the cameras. Milos and Universal insisted that a stunt man be used. Carrey, who, like Tom Cruise, prides himself on doing his own stunts, vehemently fought that decision. I sat in on a meeting between Milos and Jim on the subject. Milos described how he would "cut away at the right moment to a crowd scene and the stunt man would come in and then he'd cut back while Lawler did the 'pile driver' to the stunt man and no one would even notice." Jim disagreed and said, "Bullshit. Everyone will notice that. Filmgoers aren't idiots. They know the cutaway masks the switch with the stunt double." Both were immovable on their positions.

Production was on hold for a couple of hours with 600 extras standing by, enjoying the free donuts at the old Olympic Auditorium in Los Angeles. As the clock and costs clicked away, the Universal lawyer and the insurance company on the film discussed it. What made matters worse was that since this was Jerry's last day and he was already pissed off, he demanded to be paid in full before he shot his last scene. This sent a message to everyone that he really was going to "pile drive" Andy/Jim and reap the press reward of hurting him. Finally, the insurance company made a ruling: the "pile driver" would be done by the stunt man, not Jim. Carrey was quite angry, but there was nothing that even the $20 million gorilla could do about it. The insurance company carries the bond on the entire film; what it says goes.

Jim played the scene and then, just at the given moment, he reluctantly stepped aside and the stunt man stood in for him and received the "pile driver" from Lawler. It's a pretty spectacular move to watch. First, Jerry lifts his opponent high in the air and then flips him upside down, holding him by his legs. With the man's head between Jerry's legs, he then himself leaps in the air, tucks his own legs in, and "pile drives" the man's head into the mat. The trained stuntman knew to tuck his head at the last moment, thus missing the impact. Jim knew the tuck also, but with the hostility in Jerry, Lawler could have easily messed up the move and seriously hurt Jim.

With the scene safely in the can and a break in the filming, everyone dropped their guard. That's when it happened. Suddenly, Andy/Jim yelled at Jerry, "How was Le Dome last night?"—then spit a hawker directly in his face. Lawler snapped, five days of insults fueling his revenge. In the blink of an eye, he violently pulled Carrey by the hair and threw him to the ground in a neck-crunching headlock. Jim went down hard, for real, and blacked out. Pandemonium broke out as Universal security tackled Lawler before he could bestow more injuries on Carrey. The 600 extras who witnessed all this were quickly ushered out of the building. Paramedics rushed in and gently lifted Jim onto a stretcher. Linda Fields (Jim's assistant) was in tears. Lynne, who dutifully was capturing all this for our documentary, was quickly accosted by Hausman, who blocked the lens with his hand and screamed at the top of his voice, "SHUT THAT CAMERA OFF! ARE YOU HAPPY NOW? JIM'S REALLY HURT." But Lynne, a graduate of the Andy Kaufman School, kept the camera rolling while holding it down by her side, appearing not to be videotaping. She had early on in production put a piece of black tape over the red light which signified that the camera was running so she could capture moments discreetly. Jim was rushed to a Los Angeles hospital. Filming came to a halt and everybody was sent home. Lynne and I jumped into my car and raced to the hospital. By the time we arrived, every major media outlet in LA was gathering. This was a big story—"Jim Carrey was seriously injured on the set of a major motion picture." Jim's manager, Eric Gold, was surrounded by cameras and was giving statements to the press saying, "Jerry Lawler acted unprofessionally and hurt my client."

Lynne and I were led into a room where we saw Jim propped up in bed with a neck brace on. He was going in and out of consciousness. Assistant Linda Fields was beside herself in tears. This was bad. Lynne and I felt awful. After all, we had been goading Jim to take risks like Andy used to and now he was seriously hurt, perhaps paralyzed for life. How would they ever conclude the film without him? Everybody was ushered out of his room except Lynne, Jim's sobbing assistant Linda, and me.

Once they all left, Linda stopped crying and started to laugh. Jim's eyes popped open, and he looked at Lynne and me and said, "Gotcha!" The son of a bitch had even fooled us. Damn, Jim was getting good at these Kaufman pranks. Real good. So was Linda. We all switched back into concern mode with Jim feigning unconsciousness when a couple of nurses came in to wheel Jim into X-ray. Jim, a real Kaufmanesque trooper, actually went through countless X-rays (and radiation) to pull off the scam, just like Andy had done. I thought back to the day Andy had called me and said, "How much radiation or chemo could a healthy person take without hurting themself?" I was reliving the past. A few hours later, the hospital released a statement saying, "There was no major injury." Still, Jim wanted to wear a neck brace like Andy himself did.

That evening, I sat with Jim, Lynne, and Dotan, Jim's bodyguard, in Jim's suite at a swanky downtown LA hotel (paid for by Universal) and flipped the TV from station to station. It was the lead story on every news outlet. Kaufman would be proud. And he was, as Jim had truly become Andy.

Over the years, many people have approached me and said if they liked the film or not. Some do, some don't. But they all agreed on one thing, and that is that Jim pulled it off. He is probably the most talented individual I've ever met. No one works harder than him. Coming from a blue-collar family, he has this extraordinary work ethic. They may pay him $20 million a picture, but he's worth every penny of it. Meeting and working closely with him has been one of the high points of my life and Lynne's.

But the greatest high point of my life will be when Andy Kaufman himself walks on stage the night of his return. I will have his original conga drums set up. Andy, I know you're reading this, please come back. Do it for me. Do it for Dr. Zmudee. I don't know where you've been all these years, and maybe you've changed your mind about returning, but you need to follow through on what you told Lynne—you'd "return in thirty years." Bask in pulling off your greatest illusion. Please join us that night. I'll have a limo waiting backstage. If you just want to pop in and wave and disappear back into obscurity, fine. Just make an appearance. PLEASE!!!

*   *   *

Ring...

B: Hello!

A: Hey, Bob. It's me, Andy.

B: What's up?

A: Guess where I spent my afternoon.

B: Where?

A: A cancer ward in San Francisco.

B: How lovely. Didn't people recognize you?

A: I did a toned-down version of Clifton, without the jacket, of course. It made me come to the realization that it's not just about faking my death, it's about faking my dying also.

B: So is it doable?

A: Oh, yeah. Getting a real person dying of cancer is definitely the way to go. For one thing, they all begin to look alike at the end. You can't even tell the men from the women.

B: So what are you going to do—ask one of them to die for you?

A: They're dying anyway. I need to appeal to their sense of humor, see if they're willing to pull off a prank with me.

B: Sense of humor? Andy, they're dying!

A: So? That's just when you might need it most. If I could find one who might already be a fan of mine, I think I could pull it off.

B: Well, when that day comes, make sure you leave me your little black book.

A: My black book ... why?

B: Because there's going to be a lot of grieving girls who are going to need a big shoulder to cry on.

CHAPTER 4

Don't Ever Leave Me Alone with People

It wasn't even 8:00 a.m. when the cast and crew started to gather around the craft service truck that sat in the parking lot of Chasen's Restaurant in Beverly Hills. We were out on location, and Chasen's, which had been closed for a number of years, was doubling as an Italian eatery where George Shapiro (Danny DeVito) first spots Clifton singing badly and humiliating members of the audience … especially me (Paul Giamatti). Suddenly the ground begins to vibrate—was this the big quake that had been predicted for years? Wrong! This was a dozen Hells Angels's motorcycles turning into Chasen's parking lot, filling the already polluted LA air with a white cloud of high octane. The sound was deafening.

The two security guards hired by Universal to keep lookie-loos away stood frozen in fear. They weren't going to tangle with this band of menacing-looking gang members. In the middle of the pack of two-wheelers, a cycle with a sidecar attached held their leader. Sitting snugly inside, slugging down Jack Daniel's and puffing on a cig, was Tony Clifton (Jim Carrey). He had hired the Hells Angels to do his bidding for the day. They would run roughshod over the whole production. Chuck Zito, president of the New York chapter of the Hells Angels, disembarked his Harley and commandeered Milos Forman's director's chair, resting his legs with kickass leather boots on Milos's TV monitor. When Milos stepped out of his nearby Winnebago with his second-in-command, Michael Hausman, to see what the commotion was all about, both men's faces turned white. Clifton stomped up to Milos and said, "You've been nixed. Me and my boys are taking over filming. You got anything to say, take it up with me, not them. Comprende? Compredevo? OK, boys, get to work!"

Soon, a Hells Angel stood behind all key personnel on the set. No one said a word. Clifton took out his script and read his lines while the Hells Angels made their movie. Milos could do nothing. No one could. The two Universal security guards wandered off, wanting no part of this. Clifton read his lines perfectly, and so did the other cast members. When the Hells Angels are directing you, you do as you're told. Oddly enough, they were quite professional.

When lunchtime came, Clifton's own catering truck showed up. "Prime rib for my men." The cast and crew were too intimidated to sit at the portable lunch tables. All they could do was stand in the background as the Angels gorged themselves on the succulent beef, baked potatoes, carrots, and dessert, all washed down with an unending supply of cold beer. Cold beer and Hells Angels go hand in hand. Those guys could drink. By the time lunch break was over, they were all pretty much sloshed. Jim's assistant, Linda Fields, began looking real good to them. She locked herself in Jim's Winnebago before it was too late.

Of course, Clifton himself had been slugging down the hard stuff—Jack Daniel's. He then brought out red spray paint and gave one can to each of his gang, and said, "Follow me." They followed him to the front of Chasen's. Clifton shook his can of paint and began to deface the building, writing slogans like "Hells Angels Eat Free" and "Clifton's Joint—Prime Rib Dinner $2.99." Now remember, Chasen's was a Hollywood landmark. Its clean white-and-green exterior always stood out as you drove by it off Beverly

Boulevard. Clifton yelled, "Attack!" On command, all of the Angels started defacing the building in red paint. Traffic began to stop and people got out of their cars. A traffic cop on his motorcycle drove by, slowed down, thought about it for a second, and wisely decided to keep on driving. NOBODY was going to stop Tony and his boys. NOBODY DARED. Fifteen minutes later, when the cans ran out of red paint, Clifton admired his handiwork. The building looked like somebody had stabbed it a thousand times. Clifton declared, "That's better. Looks more like home."

Afterward, as Tony and his gang walked back to the parking lot, Milos had a shit-eating smile on his face and his own card to play. He approached Clifton and said, "Tony, I want you to meet a fellow colleague. He's a great admirer of yours … Elton John." Sure enough, standing there was the real Elton John. Tony said, "Bullshit … he's not Elton John," playing as if it was a look-alike. Milos said, "No, it's the real Elton John." Elton stood there, totally intimidated by Clifton and the surrounding Hells Angels. Clifton said, "I'll be the judge of that," then quickly turned to Elton and said, "What was the single on the *Captain Fantastic* album?" Elton, surrounded by the muscular Angels in their leathers, was thrown and couldn't remember. Clifton immediately jumped back in, "You see—it's not him." Milos insisted that it was. "OK, I'll give him one last chance. Don't go breaking my heart?" Elton timidly replied, "I won't go breaking your heart." Clifton laughed. "OK, that's him." Everybody around laughed.

Now here's what I think came down that day. Elton, who is an old friend of Milos's, happened to be in town doing a concert. Milos told him how he was directing Carrey and how Carrey had totally immersed himself in the role of Clifton, and he should come down to the set and take a look. Milos, a power schmoozer, probably figured he'd kill two birds with one stone: first he'd impress Jim that he knew Elton, and then he'd impress Elton that he was directing Jim. I'm sure Jim knew in advance that Elton was coming to the set, but no way was Elton John going to upstage Tony

Clifton, not on his own turf. So I feel Clifton needed some moral support—thus he hired the Hells Angels for the day. Lynne disagrees with my theory. She thinks Clifton just wanted to show Milos who was boss. Elton John was just a tasty hors d'oeuvre for Clifton to chew up and spit out.

Months later, Milos told me that Elton had told him that Clifton was the "most intimidating person he ever met in his life." To me, Tony and the Hells Angels defacing Chasen's were just little things that Jim used to stay in character. Constantin Stanislavski would be proud. And Milos, if nothing else, is a real "method actor" kind of director. I'm told that when they were casting *One Flew Over the Cuckoo's Nest*, he would audition his actors by having them sit in with real psychos in a nearby mental institution. He would then bring in members of his staff to try to guess who were the real nutcases and who weren't. When the staff would think that one of the cases was real when it wasn't, Milos gave that actor the job. So Milos had no problem with Jim's approach. Whatever it took to get the job done.

*   *   *

One of the most bizarre practices that Andy Kaufman took part in was "intestinal flossing." It's an old Hindu cleansing technique employed by yogi masters. It entails slowly swallowing thirty feet of cheesecloth about two inches wide, soaked in warm water with lemon juice, until the end protrudes out of one's rectum—and then one gently flosses by gripping both ends of the cloth. The idea is to clean out the entire gastrointestinal tract (approximately thirty feet long). Andy would do this to himself religiously twice a year.

We shared this delicate information with Jim, who fortunately decided to pass on this particular Kaufman ritual. Clifton did, however, share the information with Elton John when he visited the set. A few days later, Sir Elton sent separate gifts to Jim, Tony, and Andy. Jim's gift consisted of a crate of fine wines. Tony's was a stack of porno magazines of fat women, along with a bottle of hand lotion. But the kicker was Andy's gift: over 200 feet of cheesecloth!

We laughed for days! Who knew that Elton John, besides being this gifted singer/songwriter, also had a wickedly great sense of humor?

It wasn't long before it all ended. The cameras stopped rolling. Our film had wrapped. Showbiz is a gypsy-like existence. Once the show is over, everyone packs up their wares and moves on to the next production, where you meet a whole new cast of characters, and the process begins all over again. For Jim, he would go on to his next film, *Me, Myself & Irene.* Lynne and I had been a recipe book for him, chock-full of Andy ingredients that Jim needed to prepare his "Kaufman stew." Once the feast was over, the book was discarded, as it should be. Again Lynne and I lost our Andy. We'd see Jim a few more times, but things were never the same. Why should they be? We never knew this new entity called Jim Carrey. He had returned to being a multimillion-dollar major celebrity, just the type of person Andy had fought his entire career not to become.

Jim over the last few years has become quite spiritual. He no longer drinks and does only healthful things for his body and mind. He is a guiding member of an organization that believes in responsibility in media. He will no longer appear in films with violence, so much so that he actually came out with a statement telling people not to go to see *Kick-Ass 2,* which he himself appeared in, telling the public it was too violent. (He shot the film before he saw the light.) He has to be applauded for his honesty in putting his money where his mouth is. The "films without violence" rule is going to severely cut down the number of scripts he receives. Besides becoming a great actor, he is on the road to becoming a great man. I like to believe that perhaps Andy's spirituality rubbed off on him.

As for Lynne and me, we keep a candle lit in the window for Andy. Hers is a remembrance of what was, while mine is a beacon leading him back.

Eighty days of psychodrama are pretty intense. Some actors like to work that way, others don't. Paul Giamatti, who played me, doesn't. A graduate of Yale University School of Drama, one of the finest in the nation, Paul just learns his lines and leaves everybody else alone. He recognizes, however, that some actors may need it and gives them their space to wig out.

Another fine actor, Gerry Becker, who played Andy's father, Stanley, would at times get into father/son role-playing with Andy (Jim). Obviously he did his homework and would yell at Andy in the dressing room, just like the real Stanley would do. Andy, not taking any shit from his dad, would yell back. The arguments would be quite heated. During one in particular, Stanley was yelling at Andy not to do the pile driver because he might get hurt, and Stanley didn't want to see him get hurt because he *loved* him. This triggered quite a volatile exchange, with Andy screaming at the top of his lungs, "TOO LATE!" The moment became so real that the makeup girl, Sheryl Ptak, broke into tears, saying it reminded her of fights with her dad.

I only wish more of that sort of thing could have been captured in *Man on the Moon,* not wasted in the dressing room. Andy's two words—"TOO LATE!"—and the emotion behind it, told you everything you needed to know about that father/son relationship. Luckily, Lynne caught the moment for our doc.

We get a unique look into Andy's childhood through the recollection of his dad, as told to Gerry. Gerry is the consummate artist. Like Jim Carrey, he leaves no stone unturned to get to the essence of any character he's playing. Therefore, when he was cast to play Stanley, who was still alive and kicking at the time, he looked forward to the opportunity to fly out to New York City and meet him.

In fact, Gerry would tell me that he spent two weeks with Stanley. To this day, he says it was probably the worst two weeks of his life. He found Stanley to be a "rage-aholic," totally "narcissistic," with a "huge ego to match." He admitted to "abusing" Andy as a

Andy and Bob searching for wrestling matches on TV.

Andy manhandling a mannequin.

Bob and Andy's father, Stanley Kaufman.

Bob cracking up basketball great Michael Jordan at a Comic Relief event.

Bob and Andy's daughter, Maria Bellu-Colonna. She has Andy's eyes.

Bob introducing Willie Nelson and his sister to President Clinton, Vice-President Gore, and his wife, Tipper.

Bob Zmuda, Billy Crystal, Senator Ted Kennedy, Whoopi Goldberg, and Robin Williams backstage at Comic Relief.

Billy Crystal, Bob Zmuda, Whoopi Goldberg, and Robin Williams. Together they have raised over 80 million dollars for Comic Relief.

Bob Zmuda and Judd Apatow. Judd's first paying job in showbiz was for Comic Relief.

Bob Zmuda receiving his first Emmy for mounting Comic Relief.

Jim Carrey with Bob and Lauren Holly. Oddly, Jim has the same birthday as Andy Kaufman, January 17th.

Paul Giamatti as Tony Clifton, Danny DeVito, and Jim Carrey. Notice Jim is wearing a neck brace.

Hugh Hefner and Tony Clifton singing together. Hef thinks it's Jim Carrey under the makeup. It's really Zmuda.

Jim Carrey as Norman Bates's mother sits with axe to the
ready in front of the "Psycho" house.

Bob Zmuda, Jim Carrey, and Paul Giamatti as Clifton on the
set of *Man on the Moon*.

Paul Giamatti as Clifton with Jim Carrey as Andy Kaufman.

Michael Stipe of R.E.M. singing with Tony Clifton to a
sold-out audience at the famous Hollywood Bowl.

Moments later, Clifton goes berserk and has to be bodily
removed by security.

Tony Clifton performing in front of 30,000 fans at the
Hangout Festival.

Tony Clifton's classic 8x10.

Bob Zmuda with a Kenya Wildlife Service Ranger and an
orphaned elephant, whose mother was killed by poachers.
(Funds raised by Andy's return will go to helping such animals.)

Bob Zmuda shaking hands with Jeff the dog in New Orleans. Comic Relief's support helped save many of New Orleans' historic "shotgun" houses, which were damaged by Hurricane Katrina, along with displaced pets.

Lynne Margulies and Andy editing *I'm From Hollywood*, which Lynne co-directed with Johnny Legend.

Bob Zmuda and Andy Kaufman on "Uncle Andy's Funhouse."

Bob and Andy causing havoc on a local kids' show.

Bob and Andy having fun in Johnny Legend's classic
"Breakfast with Blassie."

Andy and Bob.

Tony Clifton on David Letterman. During the commercial break, Letterman turned to Tony and said, "Andy, if I didn't know it was you, I'd swear it was somebody else." It was somebody else. It was Zmuda.

Tony Clifton interviewing Bob Gorski (Zmuda).

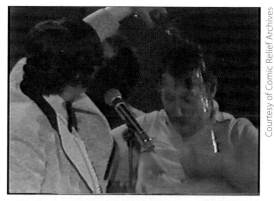

Tony, not liking what he hears, pours water over Bob Gorski (Zmuda).

Andy with Bob playing his sleazy lawyer.

The Maharishi, who gave Andy the secret of how to fake his death: "Timing."

Andy with the love of his life, Lynne Margulies.

Lynne Margulies and Andy. Notice the smile on
Andy's face. He's with his "soul mate."

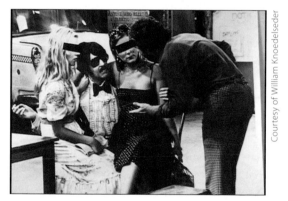

Tony Clifton on the set of *Taxi* drunk with two hookers. Judd Hirsch pleads with him to leave.

Tony Clifton being thrown off the Paramount lot by
security.

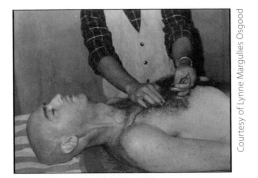

Fake surgeon. Fake blood. And fake cancer patient (Andy). This picture, taken in the Philippines, was leaked to the National Enquirer to fool the American public into thinking Andy was dying.

Lynne and Andy in the Philippines.

Zmuda and Andy, together on stage at their historic concert where they took the entire audience out on buses for milk and cookies. Is Bob also producing Kaufman's return?

Tony Clifton with two bombshells. Clifton had sex with the brunette, porn star Chasey Lain, fifteen minutes after this photo was taken. Tony said, "She was good. I was better."

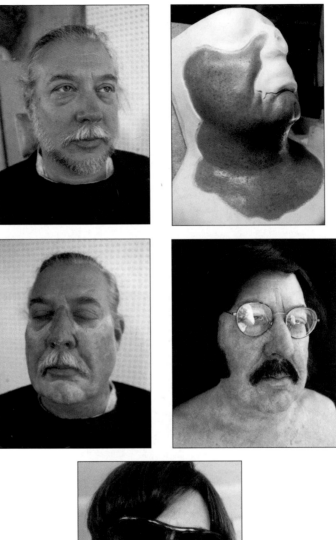

Zmuda is transformed into Tony Clifton through the use of prosthetics, the same procedure Kaufman used on his body double to fake his death.
(Makeup by Gabe Bartalos)

young boy—not physically, never physically, but psychologically. Stanley admitted that he was disappointed that Andy was not very athletic as a youngster. Stanley dreamed that his first-born would be a great athlete. Instead, Andy would just stand out in left field daydreaming as the balls flew over his head. Stanley was bipolar, and when his mood swings would kick in, he would charge up to little Andy's room and berate him horribly. Is it any wonder that Andy's only escape from such an abusive parent was to transport himself to an imaginary world where he would talk to the wall of his bedroom, believing a camera was inside and he could enchant its countless friendly viewers with his talent? That this little boy's only escape from such a tormenting dad was his own imagination is a testament to the endurance of the human spirit. Stanley would cry to Gerry and be apologetic for the hurt he'd leveled on his first-born one minute, and then begin yelling about him the next as if he were still alive.

One day, Stanley convinced Gerry that they should drive out to the family home in Great Neck so Gerry could get "a feel of the family's dwelling place." Gerry pointed out that "other people live there now and might not be so receptive to us tramping around what was now their home." Stanley replied, "Nonsense. I'm Andy Kaufman's father. They're going to be delighted to meet me." When they arrived at the home, they knocked on the door and Stanley explained to the owner who he was and that Gerry was the actor that was going to portray him and they had come to walk around inside the home. The owner said, "I think you're out of your fucking mind and get off my property." Once back in the car, Stanley started raging about how insulted he was. "Doesn't he know who I am?" Gerry chimed in, "The guy could give a shit. The world doesn't revolve around you, Stanley."

This was also the attitude Stanley had about Hollywood, that they would need him to make the movie. Gerry, not one to be intimidated by Stanley, would tell him, "The movie is not about you. It's about Andy. You need to be supportive and not get in the way." Stanley wouldn't hear any of it. The movie should be about him and Andy as a little boy, and the studio needed to know this. After another week of this nonsense, Gerry couldn't take it any more and flew back to LA

Gerry said it would have been better if Stanley were an alcoholic or taking drugs, anything to help him overcome his deep rage. Unfortunately, his hatred of the film was passed on to his other children, Michael and Carol, who showed up on the set also with a chip on their shoulder. To them, everybody working on the film was suspect. Today they still view everyone as the enemy. The enemy who stole the limelight from Stanley and themselves.

Unfortunately, such domestic abuse is multi-generational. Stanley's father was abusive to him, so Stanley was abusive to Andy. Now Stanley's children continue the trend by being abusive to those of us who try to keep Andy's legacy alive. But they need to know we're not little kids talking to the wall. We're adults with careers in the entertainment industry, careers that helped shape Andy's. It's not just Andy's work they're censoring. As his writer for ten years, I can tell you a lot of it is mine also. All I can say to them is what Gerry said to Stanley: "The legend is not about you, it's about Andy."

A funny example of Stanley's out-of-control ego is when he met his match with another diva such as himself, Babs. Or to us mere mortals, Barbra Streisand. The occasion was the 1995 Emmy Awards. My Shapiro-West NBC special, *A Comedy Salute to Andy Kaufman*, was nominated for best TV special. As the executive producers, George Shapiro, Howard West, John Davies, and myself were invited guests. We decided to invite Stanley, knowing that such an occasion would be a thrill for him. One of the other specials nominated was HBO's Barbra Streisand special.

As I was settling into my seat at the Shrine Auditorium, Howard West tapped me on the shoulder and said, "We just lost." I said, "What do you mean we just lost? The presentation hasn't even begun." Howard said, "Streisand just walked in." I said, "So? The nominating committee keeps the winner secret until the envelopes are opened live on the air." Howard said, "That's all bullshit. I'm telling you, Babs wouldn't be here unless she already knew she won. They want her here for the ratings."

Howard, George's partner, was an old, savvy master of how the Hollywood game was played. He was right, and the room lit up when later in the evening, Streisand was announced the winner. Acting totally surprised, she majestically rose and walked to the dais to receive the golden man with wings, the coveted Emmy. Howard poked me in the ribs and said, "See? I told you so, kid!"

After the Emmy celebration, they have what is called the Governors Ball. It's a high-end dinner usually catered by Wolfgang Puck. The seating arrangement is such that you are grouped together with the other nominees in your particular category. Since ours was TV specials, it was no surprise that we found our table next to Streisand's. In fact, the back of my chair faced the back of Babs's.

Stanley couldn't believe our luck and at one point in the evening, whispered in my ear to ask if it would be acceptable for him to introduce himself to Streisand. I whispered back, "Yes, but wait for her stooges to leave the table," as there were two PR people of hers seated on each side, flanking her from anyone who even thought of approaching the "living legend." Stanley waited a good hour for the opportunity. In the interim, he really started tossing back the champagne. He was not a heavy drinker, and soon the bubbly got to his brain and he was pretty inebriated when Streisand's guards finally left her, if only for a few minutes. During this window of vulnerability, Stanley moved in. Being Stanley, he sat down right next to her. She was appalled. Stanley, who was nervous and drunk, started slurring his words and babbling on about how he was Andy Kaufman's dad and if his son was going to lose, at least it was to a nice Jewish girl from Brooklyn. Streisand wasn't having any of it. I don't even think she knew or cared who Andy Kaufman was. She just wanted this drunk gone and looked around desperately for her handlers. They arrived a short time later, but not before Stanley had the audacity to place his arm around the back of her chair. Her PR people quickly ushered him away, not too delicately. I couldn't help but laugh as I heard the lyrics of one of her greatest hits run through my head …

"PEOPLE … PEOPLE WHO NEED PEOPLE …

ARE THE LUCKIEST PEOPLE IN THE WORLD …"

… as she screamed at her henchmen, "Don't ever leave me alone with *PEOPLE!*"

*   *   *

Richard Belzer said it best: "Andy Kaufman was a provocateur." Stanley was less French about it: "The kid's a troublemaker." I think a lot of Andy's shtick grew out of his wanting a way to irritate his father. Could that be it? Could all this highfalutin' talk of enigmatic anti-comedy performance art be a bunch of hyperbole? Did Father Know Best? "Troublemaker." Had the Kaufmans not been such upscale Jews with the finances to send a child to a shrink, but instead had been a blue-collar goyim family where old man Stanley would have put that kid across his lap and taken his belt to him, I wouldn't have to be sitting here some sixty years later trying to make sense of it all. "Spare the whip, spoil the child." Abusive? Stanley may have been too tolerant of a dad. And then to make matters worse, Andy's bad behavior brings him fame and fortune. Christ! They even make a major motion picture about him. To Stanley, the world must have gone mad, rewarding the troublemaker. It's all one big misunderstanding. Streisand knows. She never heard of him. She's got real talent. That's why she got the Emmy and his "troublemaking" son did not.

Honestly, what did the family think? Universal had cast Jim Carrey. Were they somehow going to shrink him down to playing an eight-year-old for three-quarters of the film so Stanley could tell his side of the story? The Kaufman family hadn't a clue as to how the film business worked. George Shapiro should have explained it to them. Maybe he tried. He was a pro and knew to keep his mouth shut. This was the big dogs spending big bucks. Stanley Kaufman didn't have a chance, because Stanley didn't have a clue what Andy was all about. He thought he did, but he didn't. In fact, I doubt any member of the Kaufman clan had ever taken the time out to explore the early 20th century Dada movement, to which Andy's work was constantly being compared. Of course the Kaufmans would hate the film—they were portrayed as bozos. I wouldn't like the film either if I were them. Who wants to be portrayed as idiots? And yet the screenwriters got it right. Andy pranked his family continually. Like it or not, that's how Andy himself cast them in relationship to his career.

*   *   *

Lynne

Andy never once talked about his "real" childhood. He would only talk about putting on shows for the imaginary camera in the wall. He did say that his parents sent him to a psychiatrist at a very young age because he seemed unhappy. But he would never tell me why he was so unhappy. He'd just say, "I don't know, I would just stare out the window and they thought something was wrong with me." When he was a teenager, he started drinking and taking drugs. He claimed that if he had not discovered Transcendental Meditation, he probably would have died. Why so unhappy as a teenager? He would never say. I now realize that Stanley must have made his life miserable as a child. His sweet mother, Janice, always seemed like a frightened little bird; it didn't occur to me at the time that it was probably because Stanley was such a brute. Andy always treated his family like it

*was a sitcom. When we visited he would revert to a false Long
Island accent, call his parents "Mommy" and "Daddy" and act
like life with his family was one long* Leave it to Beaver *episode.
All make-believe and fun. Never serious; harsh words were never
spoken. I wonder now if this was to cover up bad memories of an
unhappy childhood. Perhaps this was the core of Andy's entire
career; making the world a "happy place" where Howdy Doody
was real, Santa Claus could actually fly in on his sleigh, and a
grown man could tinker at the piano singing children's songs
and become famous for it. When Andy and Bob created Tony
Clifton, was Andy perhaps impersonating his father Stanley?*

Lynne's insight into the origin of Clifton may be spot on. I know
a lot of the brutality Clifton displays when I play him comes from
my own father.

Another valuable insight into Stanley Kaufman's "explosive
personality" may be war-related PTSD (post-traumatic stress disorder). According to Dr. Joseph Troiani, an expert in the field,
"Those who have been in combat [Stanley Kaufman was awarded
three Purple Hearts for injuries he sustained in World War II] have
a tendency for aggressive and violent behavior once they return
home stateside." Unfortunately, the Veterans Administration did
not take PTSD seriously until after the Vietnam War. Poor Stanley,
a bona fide war hero, suffered in silence and couldn't help inflict-
ing his torments on his children and wife. I'm a big believer in
a "sins of the father" psychology. Could Andy's own aggressive
behavior played out on national television be a direct link to the
trauma Stanley experienced in northern France? Could Tony Clifton's unruly behavior actually be PTSD left over from World War II?

Lynne's comment that "Andy never talked about his past"
is also insightful. I found that to be true when he nonchalantly
mentioned one day he had a daughter who he'd never met. I was
dumbfounded. Years after his supposed death, his daughter, Maria,
surfaced. It seemed that Andy at sixteen knocked her mother up in

high school. He was prepared to marry her when the Kaufmans and the girl's parents interceded and said the teenagers were too young to get married. It was decided the child would be put up for adoption. Once an adult, Maria tracked down her biological mom, who told her that her father was the late Andy Kaufman. Kaufman had never mentioned another word about it to me, and I knew I'd better not ask.

*   *   *

Andy and I prided ourselves on being able to manipulate the media. In fact, Kaufman is equally recognized for the routines he pulled offstage as on. Therefore, I must admit I was quite impressed with the Universal Studios publicity department when they announced that the press campaign for our film would be twofold. First they would do the traditional press, but more important, because of the subject matter, namely Andy Kaufman, they wanted also to mount a non-traditional press campaign; i.e., guerrilla tactics, which of course was right up my alley. Still, it was Universal Studios, so I was at first skeptical as to how guerrilla they were willing to go.

I was flabbergasted when one day I was summoned to Universal's "Black Tower" to meet with the head of the publicity department. His name was Marc Shmuger. I entered his office, cordially shook hands, and sat down. He said, "This conversation never took place. Bob, our research shows us [waving his hand toward a stack of field reports and journals] that there is a strong possibility that hard-core Kaufman zealots might turn on this film, for no other reason than we're a major motion-picture company wanting to make a 'commercial' film of their anti-hero. They don't trust us. We need to become the 'good guys' by first of all becoming the 'bad guys.' So here's what we're going to do with your help. We are going to set up a phony website with imaginary die-hard Kaufman fans. They will attack our own film. They will attack you."

"Me?" I said.

"Yes, for this site to be believable to Kaufman fans, and so they won't suspect it's us, we need you to be our sacrificial lamb. Our website will paint you as a sellout for agreeing to produce commercial slop. We'll say that we heard the script is godawful and an insult to Andy's memory."

I swallowed hard, still baffled. "I'm a sellout?" Marc said, "Well, just at first, of course. Once they believe the site's for real, we'll slowly turn everything around. Show them the script, which of course they'll love because we'll be telling them how great it is." All I could repeat was, "I'm a sellout?" Marc said, "Of course we'll soon turn that around too. In a few weeks, they'll love you again and everyone associated with the film."

I looked around his office, walls hung with posters of successful Universal films. All I could utter was my best impression of Richard Dreyfuss in *Close Encounters of the Third Kind* when he said, "Who are you people?" Marc laughed. I then said, "Why would I possibly want to be your sacrificial lamb? What if the whole thing backfires? What do I get out of it?" Marc said, "Good question. You get what you and Andy always wanted: a career for Tony Clifton." My ears perked up and I said, "Go on. I'm listening."

"Jimmy Miller [Carrey's manager] told us that Jim's schedule doesn't allow him to do much promotion for the film. So we figure, Who's the next best thing? TONY CLIFTON." He then undraped an easel. Under it was a large poster board with a heading that read, "Tony Clifton Publicity Campaign." Underneath were bullet points indicating photo shoots, TV appearances, a TV pilot, a national tour, etc. Andy and I dreamed of getting Tony out there in a major way, and now here it was laid out in front of me by the head of publicity of a major studio, and bankrolled on top of that. Someone pinch me! Marc said, "What do you say? Will you be our sacrificial lamb?" I immediately started to "Baaaa ..." I left his office flying on a cloud, but also thinking, "I'll never believe anything I ever read or see on the news again. Big Brother's for real."

Immediately, they lined up a major photo shoot with one of the top Hollywood photographers, Wayne Williams. In the photos were two hot babes. One was porn star Chasey Lain. Seeing that I was in the Clifton disguise and this was a shoot for *Man on the Moon,* she assumed, like Hugh Hefner, that underneath all the prosthetics I was wearing, I must be Jim Carrey in disguise. I didn't let her think otherwise. During one of the breaks, I took her into one of the back rooms, where she was more than eager to give it up. Wayne Williams's photos were to run in all the major publications: *Variety, Hollywood Reporter, Entertainment Weekly,* etc. Full-page color.

Next we shot an entire pilot for a series. It was called *Judge Tony.* I came up with the idea of a *Judge Judy*-like show, but in this case (no pun intended) the judge would be fake but the litigants would be real and wouldn't know Tony was fake, and he would be like the worst judge in the world. The show's producer hung out at an LA courthouse in front of the small-claims court, and real people with real cases were selected. We wanted cases that were clear-cut as to who was right and who was wrong. Of course Judge Tony always called it wrong. The litigants were told that they would be paid for appearing on TV. Monies would be awarded to the winner of the case, and they could also still go back to small-claims court. The producers rented a real-looking courtroom in Culver City.

Clifton was outrageous. In one case, a large, middle-aged Russian woman who had only received her citizenship six months before was threatened with deportation when she couldn't recite the Pledge of Allegiance, as Clifton demanded—proof enough to Judge Tony that she was a "commie bastard." The woman ran out to her car in tears. Luckily, one of the producers was able to calm her down before she pulled away, letting her know it was a put-on. The pilot was hysterically funny, some of Clifton's best work.

The studio was also supportive of Clifton's putting a band together and going out on tour across the U.S. in conjunction with the release of the film. I called my old friend Billy Swan to be musical director. Billy had a hit in 1974 with the song "I Can Help." He also was a musician in Kris Kristofferson's band and a close friend of his. Andy and I met Billy and Kris when we did a political whistle-stop tour for Gov. Jerry Brown's election. That tour was insane. Kristofferson was a matinee film idol at the time, and women would follow our tour bus up and down the coast of California, with Kristofferson inside. When we pulled into some roadside motel at night, the women would sit parked in their cars waiting for Kris to step out on his balcony. When he did, they all suddenly left their vehicles and stood next to them, so Kristofferson could get a look at the goods. Every night, he'd summon one or two up to his room. Andy would be jealous and sexually frustrated as all hell watching Kris's behavior and complain, "That dorky Latka character sends the wrong message to women. I wish I never had invented him. I should have brought along a hooker or two." Andy would stay up half the night flipping through the yellow pages under "Escort Services" looking for some "companionship."

Anyway, I called up Billy, and he assembled a top-notch band of well-known studio musicians from Memphis. Tony flew down there, and he had a great time rehearsing. Eventually, we even cut a few songs at Sun Records and recorded in the same room that Elvis, Johnny Cash, and Jerry Lee Lewis did—the bathroom. No joke. At Sun Records, the most acoustically balanced room in the whole place is this tight, one-seat crapper. And all the greats recorded many a hit while sitting on it. Tony could now add his name to a long list of recording stars who had done the same.

When the band and Tony were ready, Billy booked Clifton at a well-known nightspot. I was in heaven. Here I was, a co-executive producer on a big-budget film starring a major actor. Paul Giamatti is playing me in the film. Tony Clifton's career is just about to launch. He has his own band, has just recorded at Sun Records, and tonight is playing at one of Memphis's hottest clubs. Too good to be true … And it was.

It started with a frantic call from Lynne to my hotel room just a couple hours before Tony was to go onstage. She was nearly in tears. "Lynne, what's wrong?" I asked. "Dr. Zmudee, you're not going to like it. I just got off the phone with Jim. I've never heard him like this before. He was yelling, demanding your phone number at the hotel." "Why?" I asked. Lynne answered, "Because he doesn't want you to do Clifton!" "What?!?" I said. "That's absurd." Lynne, herself distraught, said she had to get off the line because Jim would be calling me momentarily. She hung up, feeling really bad for me, knowing my dream had come to a screeching halt.

No sooner did I hang up than my phone rang again. I took a deep breath and picked it up, believing it to be Jim. It wasn't. It was Marc Shmuger, Universal's chief of publicity. His news was worse than Lynne's. Marc elaborated, telling me that Jim had flipped out and killed the entire Tony Clifton campaign—magazine ads, Judge Tony, the record, the live tour … EVERYTHING. Marc ended by saying, "I'm really sorry, Bob. I know how much this meant to you. But Jim's an eight-hundred-pound gorilla. My hands are tied." And PUFF! Just like that, it was over. The Lord God giveth, and the Lord God taketh away. The Lord God was Jim Carrey.

By the time Jim called, I was pretty despondent. I just couldn't believe it. I thought he was my friend. The voice on the other end of the phone, which was screaming in my ear, almost didn't resemble Jim, as I had never seen or heard this side of him before. He started to cut me a new asshole. He told me that I "was fucking everything up." My having my Clifton out there was going to be confusing to the public when the movie came out. Obviously he wanted to be the new image of Clifton in the public mind, especially if this film was a hit. Who knew if he'd be offered another film playing Tony? (Remember, Universal still owned the rights to *The Tony Clifton Story*, which was sitting in the Universal vault gathering dust.)

Arrogance or truth came out (you take your pick) when he lambasted me and then turned on Andy for not having nearly the career that he now had. "Bob, Andy's career was never at the level of mine," he said. "This picture is going to make him bigger. You too. Don't screw it up." He could feel my pain and softened just a little at the end. "Look, Dr. Zmudee," he said. "Let's get this film behind us, and later down the road, I'll help you with Clifton." All I could murmur was, "You promise?" "I promise," he said, and then hung up.

I was totally devastated. Remember, I still loved the guy. So did Lynne. To us, he was Andy. Of course, not the real Andy, but the next best thing. Those eight years, two shows a night at The Comedy Store for free had left their mark. He'd paid his dues, and nothing and nobody was going to grab that brass ring out of his tightly clenched fist. There was little I could do. Still, I had my own history of paying my dues. Besides, I also had Tony Clifton in my corner, the real Tony Clifton. A month later, Clifton planned his revenge on the superstar, and his $20 million per pic didn't mean squat.

Seeing that Jim's management made it clear that his schedule would not allow much time for promotion, it was decided that his big PR commitment would be one day—but what a day it would be. It would be the largest promotional day, not only for *Man on the Moon,* but also for other studio films and their stars. It was called a press junket and was to be held at the famous Four Seasons Hotel in Beverly Hills. The studios would rent out three floors of rooms for journalists, both domestic and foreign, lavishly treat them to drinks and fine foods, and then starting at 9:00 a.m., parade the stars from one journalist to another. Even Lynne and I were summoned in to talk to the press.

Of course the big event of the junket was the appearance of Jim Carrey, the highest-paid star in Hollywood. For such an auspicious occasion, they rented out the largest and most lavish banquet room in the hotel and filled it to the max with photographers, video operators, and journalists. While the journalists were seated in comfortable silk-back chairs with chandeliers hanging over their heads, Jim was seated alone up front at a long table loaded with microphones and tape recorders belonging to those gathered. As he diligently answered their questions, little did he know that Tony Clifton had snuck into the building and, *à la* Sirhan Sirhan, was taking the service elevator down to Jim's floor. Though the studio had security at the entrance of the banquet room to keep uninvited guests out, there was no one guarding the service elevator that led directly into the kitchen and then into the interview room. Clifton was on a mission: "Fuck with my career, Carrey, I'm gonna fuck with yours!"

Soon, the elevator doors opened and in entered the real Tony Clifton, the international singing sensation lounge lizard who Jim Carrey had tried to put an end to. Clifton was not happy and stormed right up the aisle to Jim. Jodee Blanco, my publicist, who knew this guerrilla attack was going to take place, nervously stood among the publicists from Universal to monitor their reaction. All of them turned white as Clifton started taunting Carrey in the most disrespectful way, yelling stuff like, "Academy Award wannabe," and "If Universal was smart, they'd change the name of the film from *Man on the Moon* to *Tony on the Moon*; then people will come see it." Clifton raged; Jim was dumbstruck. For the first time in his entire career, he didn't know what to do or say. He might be the 800-pound gorilla, but Clifton is the 8,000-pound Kong. This was no match.

Tony had decided the great Jim Carrey was going down, and down he went, big-time. He couldn't put two words together. Before he knew it, Clifton pulled out a can of black spray paint. He approached the luxurious French felt flowered wallpaper pattern behind him, shook the aerosol and started to spray in large black letters the words "Tony on the Moon" while yelling to the press that HE, not Carrey, should be nominated for his portrayal of himself in the film. While Clifton defaced the premises, the press nervously laughed along, thinking, "That wall's going to cost a pretty penny." Jim now realized he had to act. He murmured something about Clifton being a drunk, but his comeback fell flat and he knew it. Trapped and knowing there was no way to top Clifton, Jim did the dumbest thing: he let his frustration get the best of him and lashed out by taking his arm and sweeping it across the table, knocking ten to fifteen tape recorders of the press onto the floor in pieces. The top Universal press woman almost had a heart attack. Jim then ran from the scene, out of the room. It was bedlam.

Next, Clifton picked up a copy of my book, *Andy Kaufman Revealed!*, and began to tear out pages, yelling, "Zmuda's book, which is now on sale in bookstores across the country, is all lies, *LIES*, I tell you." Next, he unzipped his pants, pulled out his pecker (prosthetic, of course, cost me a pretty penny too, $150—goodness, you didn't think *I* would expose my family jewels—heavens!), and began to urinate on the manuscript. Another Universal press person nearly fainted. People began to scatter as the "urine"-spewing Clifton began to run up and down the aisle wielding his dick like a squirt gun. This was a nightmare!

By now, in some back room, Jim had composed himself and knew he wasn't going to leave it with Clifton's running him out of his own press conference. So he grabbed a huge pitcher of ice water, rushed out and up to Clifton, and doused him with it, yelling, "You're all wet." Clifton was stunned and immobilized by the freezing slosh. The press loved that, and Jim got a huge laugh and even applause out of it, which is all he really wanted. And then Jim went his way and Tony went his, leaving the battered and broken tape recorders, soaked in Clifton's piss (apple juice, Mott's brand), strewn across the floor.

Boy, did Clifton get me in trouble on that one. Jodee Blanco attended an "emergency" damage-control meeting with Universal in putting together a press release. She recalls her experiences that morning:

What a day, good grief! I knew things would go from bad to worse the moment I entered Bob's hotel suite to escort him to the junket. I stepped into the ladies' room to check my lipstick, and screamed. There, sitting on the bathroom counter, was this large, flesh-toned penis complete with hairs and wrinkles, and attached at the base was a long tube. "Zmuuuuda! What the HELL is this, oh my God!" He giggled and said, "That's for Tony; really lifelike, don't you think?" He started to tell me what he planned on doing with it, and I stopped him, not wanting to know. In that moment, I felt my twenty-year successful career careening into a wall. I begged him not to use the dildo. "Aw, come on, Jodee, it's for Andy," he said. "The studio and Jim are getting cold feet with all this Kaufmanesque stuff, and I need to do this for my friend," he begged. "If the situation were reversed, Andy would do it for me. Please, Jodee, don't tell Universal." I reluctantly acquiesced. Part of me thought Jim was in on the prank, so I figured, when it's all said and done, everything will be fine, because it had Jim's blessing. Wrong. I'll never forget that emergency meeting afterwards. Bob and Jim both had exited the building, leaving me holding the bag. The head of publicity and several other suits grabbed my arm and hustled me into one of their suites at the hotel. We all sat down and whipped out our notebooks and laptops. "OK, so how do we spin this?" their publicity director asked. "Jodee, how do we position the penis?" It was the single most surreal moment of my career. I've since gotten out of publicity. Can you blame me?

Clifton and Zmuda were summarily barred from the Universal lot, and Tony is still blacklisted to this day from all Four Seasons Hotels. Universal bought new tape recorders to replace the ones that had been destroyed and had to pay to re-wallpaper the ballroom wall. But at the end of the day, the press hit from it was phenomenal for the film. Andy would have been proud, even if Universal wasn't.

As far as Jim was concerned, I'm sure he thought Clifton did it for the publicity. He didn't. Clifton wanted to rain on Jim's parade just like Jim had rained on Tony's. Still, it was hard for me to hold a grudge against Jim. I love the guy, and anybody who ever really knows him loves him too. But for Lynne and me, for eighty days, while working on the film, it was like having Andy back. Literally.

Jim, if nothing else, is a pro. It's no wonder he was the high-est-paid performer in Hollywood. He's worth it. He simply works harder than anyone else. He left no stone unturned in his research on Kaufman. He devoured everything and would constantly download Lynne and me about Andy. Of course, we never told him about Andy being bisexual. We feared it might scare Jim away from the project or tilt the film in a certain direction. We didn't want "the bisexuality" to overpower everything he already knew about an already enigmatic character such as Kaufman. Besides, we didn't know how DeVito would take it, let alone Milos and the studio. So Lynne and I just kept our mouths shut about the subject. Andy's dad Stanley was still alive, and one of Andy's dying wishes was that we not breathe a word about it while his parents were alive. His mom was still alive when Andy "died." As Tony Clifton waxed poetically, "Stanley was able to pass peacefully away never knowing his son was a cocksucker and pooper scooper!"

After the Four Seasons incident, Universal thought I had totally lost my mind. All their original talk about supporting a guerrilla-type campaign was just that: talk. Getting close to the release date, with everyone nervous, they were running scared. I was told that I was not allowed even to attend the premiere of my own film unless I promised I would not pull another Clifton stunt. In fact, the night of the premiere, they hired a guard to follow me wherever I went. I was even taken into a back room of the theater and cavity-searched, making sure I wasn't hiding a Tony Clifton wig, mustache, or sunglasses up my keester. Only then was I allowed into the venue.

*   *   *

Lynne

I got tarnished with the Clifton brush even though I had had nothing to do with the press-junket incident. At the New York premiere, Courtney Love pulled me into the women's room at the theater and gave me a rambling lecture about how Clifton was ruining Man on the Moon's *chances for being a hit and that she did not want to see her good friend Milos suffer. I could only tell her that Clifton was his own man and there was nothing I, or anyone else, could say or do that could influence him. It was Clifton, after all. They had just made a movie about Andy and Clifton, didn't they get it? This was all par for the course, but then, Hollywood could never, not ever, take something to the edge of sanity the way Andy and Bob would. There is too much money involved. They can say that they "get it," but when push comes to shove, they will always cave. Not Andy. He never once "winked" at the audience to give them the relief of knowing it was all a joke. That is what his art was all about, and that is what* Man on the Moon *should have been about. How innocent of Bob and me to think that it could have been otherwise. Hollywood will always "wink." Somehow I think we believed that they wouldn't because they were making a film about the great purist, Andy Kaufman.*

*   *   *

If there was ever a film that cried out for a non-traditional advertising campaign, it was *Man on the Moon.* After all, Andy Kaufman's entire career was based on manipulating the media. I know because that is just what Andy and I did for ten years. Be it faking his neck injury, hoodwinking the public as to Tony Clifton's true identity, or faking his death, it was all the same—the goal was to pull the wool over the eyes of the American public, and by so doing garner large amounts of free press.

Since Jim Carrey and his people made it clear to Universal from the get-go that Jim was not going to be able to do much press for the film because of his demanding schedule, they needed to pursue other angles of publicity. From the very first publicity meeting, everybody knew this, but at some point the publicity department lost its way. One could hardly blame them after Marc Shmuger took a leap of faith and decided to build a campaign around Tony Clifton, only to have his head handed to him by Jim himself. The height of folly came when I managed to secure the cover of *Esquire* magazine with Jim as Andy and Tony Clifton on it. I even got Jim to sign off on it, which was no small accomplishment. I was flabbergasted when the idea was rejected by Jersey Films and Universal's publicity department. I hit the roof. Here they had no campaign themselves and—thanks to the assistance of Bill Zehme—I get the cover of a major publication and they reject it? OK, I could see them rejecting Clifton's antics, but here was a traditional campaign, securing a major publication with the star signed, sealed, and delivered, and they still said no.

At that point I realized we were out on open seas with no one at the helm. Without a solid publicity campaign, a film, no matter how good it is, doesn't have a chance of attracting an audience. *Man on the Moon* was dead in the water before it even got released. And then to add insult to injury, Jersey Films decided to open the film at Christmastime. Originally we were scheduled for Thanksgiving, when we would have been the only film out there. But somebody got greedy and thought we could become the big Christmas movie, which pitted us against other major studios. I called up everybody pleading with them not to release us for Christmas. We weren't that type of film. Kaufman himself was never a mainstream act. He was cultish. Fans had to discover him. He couldn't be forced down their throats. I managed to get George Shapiro and Milos on my side, but both men had no fight left in them.

If there's a lesson to be learned, it's this: No matter what, stick to your guns. Keep fighting for what you believe in—even if you become a pest. I surely was. Years later, Stacey Sher, who broke from DeVito and ventured out on her own, producing such hits as *Django Unchained,* told me, "Looking back, I now realize we were wrong not backing you on your publicity concepts for the film. It's as if we were acting just like Stanley Kaufman, not supporting Andy."

I could only laugh. I wish I had a nickel for every time Clifton has been hired for a gig and the buyers think they want those antics. But nine times out of ten, once Tony starts pushing the envelope, they get nervous about it and chicken out. Especially nowadays, with this liberal political-correctness standard that aims to make sure that nobody is offended. If you can't offend people in a free society, then the question you have to ask yourself is, "Just how free is it?" I'm proud of the fact that today Tony Clifton advertises his show by saying, "At least five N-words per show or your money back." Michael Kaufman is offended by Clifton's behavior. In fact, he refers to him nowadays as "the vile Tony Clifton." Vile Tony Clifton? Isn't that redundant? Michael tried being Clifton once—it didn't work. It's not his fault, he's just too nice of a guy. Let's call his Tony "the milquetoast Tony Clifton."

To play Tony Clifton, one has to adhere to strict guidelines laid down by Andy himself:

1. You must consume large amounts of alcohol (preferably Jack Daniel's).
2. You must eat meat. (Andy and I are both vegetarians.)
3. Hookers, hookers, and more hookers.
4. Language—as filthy as you can muster.
5. The most important: Clifton must never *ever* censor himself. Whatever thoughts pop into his alcohol-fueled head must immediately come right out of his mouth, just as if he had Tourette's.

People who attend Clifton's shows are at first shocked. Nobody would dare say the things Clifton says. But as the night wears on, the audience sees that Clifton is an equal-opportunity offender. And, like Archie Bunker, his pathos eventually wins them over. I cannot think of any performance where he hasn't received a standing ovation. As one critic said, "Don't miss Clifton. It's the closest you'll ever get to seeing an Andy Kaufman performance."

Well, that will all change when the original returns. Andy, I wonder if you have a gut nowadays or are you still going to need the fake stomach to wear when you play Tony?

*   *   *

In the end, *Man on the Moon* was a bust, grossing $47 million worldwide with a production budget of over $80 million. Having dabbled in screenwriting myself, I understand the challenges inherent in telling Andy's story for the screen, especially as he was one of the most elusive performers of our time. To infuse his philosophy of "I think of the world as an illusion and we shouldn't take ourselves so seriously" in every scene, while including the many highlights of his illustrious career, all the while maintaining a believable story line that moves the audience to both laughter and tears, while preserving the nobility of Kaufman, is a tall order, and Scott and Larry remarkably pulled it off. Considering that, statistically, the average movie audience is male teenagers and their dates, what were DeVito, Ron Meyer, and Stacey Snider thinking in the first place? You can't do a successful commercial film about Kaufman.

When Lynne first met Scott and Larry, who were writing the script, she told them that it was an impossible task. There was nothing "cinematic" about Andy's life that would fit into the standard Hollywood format. But it was Universal's money so what the hell, give it a try. It might be crazy enough to work. And honest to God, I think they pulled it off. Even though the film was not a box-office hit when it was released, that does not overshadow its effectiveness today. People love this movie. I know that because I've been hearing that every week from fans since its release in 1999. Because of broadcasts, DVD sales, Netflix, etc., the film now has a loyal following, continues to grow its audience, and is no doubt instrumental in building Kaufman mania to new heights. Since the film's release, I've seen a new audience of young people flocking to see Clifton in concert and fascinated by Andy. So Danny DeVito, you're forgiven in my book. I'm willing to bury the hatchet if you are.

Danny not only made *Man on the Moon* as a "labor of love," but also from a psychological imperative in him that ran deep, deep in his psyche—which was "absolution." He loved Andy. You can tell it in his portrayal of Andy's manager, George Shapiro. You could tell it every moment he was on the set producing "his" film of Andy's life. He and Jim brought Andy back. Realistically, all the political backstabbing behind the scenes still couldn't take away from the fact that DeVito pulled it off. Amazingly, he gathered almost the entire cast of *Taxi* back together and basically rubbed their and his own face in the fact that they had been working with a genius all those years ago and had belittled that fact. Some of them got it; some didn't. Carol Kane, who is a sweetheart, loved Andy so much she was the only one to show up at his funeral. Jeff Conaway, who couldn't stand Andy when he was alive, probably came around the most, realizing he had totally blown it. He said apologetically, "First time around, I was emotionally involved. You were an unwitting player. I couldn't divorce myself from the situation. If I had, I could have enjoyed myself. Making *Man on the Moon* is a trip—stranger than any acid trip I ever took."

Marilu Henner, a fellow Chicagoan whom I've had the pleasure of knowing for over forty-five years, pretty much stayed out of the fray. Her take on Andy hits the nail right on the head: "He was an absolute original, a thoroughly fascinating, unfathomable, complex, uncompromised, talented artist who marched through his short, strange life to a very different drummer." Tony Danza wasn't available for the filming, or so we were told. Maybe he knew of DeVito's journey into darkness and wanted no part of it.

Judd Hirsch did show up and probably wished he hadn't. He was the most silent during the filming and probably in real life liked Andy the least. Jim Carrey knew this and had Clifton needle him whenever he could. Judd's take on the whole ordeal was, "I don't know why we're here. We're not doing anything here that's worthwhile. We're dealing with a maniac! He [Andy] used to be an annoying guy, but now, when it's all said and done, he needs to leave the earth. There's no room for people like that, certainly not in show business—not the show business I came from." In all fairness to Judd, I wasn't sure if he was acting when he said this or if it's how he really felt. Or maybe he was smart enough to figure out how Danny wanted him to be portrayed. Lynne's take is that he was acting; although he didn't like Andy much during the *Taxi* days, in this case he was in character. Remember, Hirsch is a top actor, real Broadway heavy-drama stuff. Throw him into a psychodrama and the surrealism of all of them playing themselves and you're in the deep end of the pool, especially Jim seeking his revenge on the *Taxi* cast in the role of Tony Clifton, who they fired in real life. And now they find themselves in a major motion picture about the guy's life. Conaway was right: "Stranger than any acid trip I ever took."

And yet this was the reality we all found ourselves in for eighty days of principal photography. Andy said it best one day on the set when he was taunting Jerry Lawler: "I'm invincible. I'm visiting from the other world, so you can't kill me!" Hopefully Jim Carrey will allow the documentary we made to be released one day. It's his finest work, and although some may think that was PR hype when they said he channeled Andy, I defy anyone to view the doc and walk away without saying that. Jim was Kaufman for real. Afterward, Jim stated that he had never in his life approached a role like that before and doubted he ever would again.

*   *   *

When I was young, one of the first showbiz jobs I had was working for a brilliant raving maniac named Norman Wexler, the famous screenwriter who penned such classics as *Saturday Night Fever* and *Serpico,* among others. In my first book, *Andy Kaufman Revealed!* (Little, Brown), I refer to him as Mr. X. (For you fans out there who always come up to me and ask who he was, now you know.) Norman would always say, "Put the right heads on the right bodies and the world blows up," meaning basically put the right pieces together and the truth emerges.

I have to thank Jeff Conaway, Andy's *Taxi* cohort, for putting my head on my right body. For years, Jeff struggled to understand the rationale behind Andy's behavior. After all, Jeff beat the hell out of Kaufman once in a drunken rage and then called Andy the next day to seriously apologize. Andy graciously accepted his apology and after that, they became friends. On the set of *Man on the Moon,* Jeff sought me out one day and said he had something very important to tell me. "Bob, it took me years to figure this out. But I now believe that Andy had no intention of Tony Clifton being on *Taxi.* [Andy had in his contract that Tony Clifton would appear in four episodes of *Taxi.* When Tony showed up for rehearsal, he was drunk and brought along two prostitutes. Eventually he was removed by security.] He caused that ruckus on the set because he wanted to be fired. He enjoyed it."

So Jeff got me thinking again. Of course Andy faked his death. What greater narcissistic martyrdom than sacrificing himself for all of tabloid journalism to see. He would lift his story line from the Greatest Book Ever Written, the Bible. Move over, Jesus, Andy's resurrection is going to be as startling as yours and on Pay-Per-View!

(Production note: Remind me to hire the Mormon Tabernacle Choir to sing Handel's "Hallelujah" chorus. Also get a "flying rig" so I can lower Kaufman down from the ceiling while they sing.)

*   *   *

So what traumatizing experience in Andy's past would trigger such behavior as to fake his death? I believe it was the death of his favorite grandfather, Papu, when he was a little boy. In that case, his parents faked his grandfather's death also. Let me explain. Before Andy would lock himself in his room and start talking to the walls (which would be unnerving to any parent), he appeared to be a normal young boy. He had a grandfather and they simply adored each other. Papu and Andy would sing songs together, play games, and just have a great time. And then one day the grandfather stopped coming around. Little Andy waited and waited. Every day, he'd stand by the window looking out. But Papu never, ever showed his face again. Andy asked his parents, "Where is he?" And here is where Stanley and Janice confess they made a horrible mistake. The grandfather had died, but they couldn't tell Andy as they thought it would break his heart. So instead, they lied and told him he went away to another country far, far across the ocean and wasn't coming back. Andy was greatly saddened that his grandfather left him without even saying goodbye and hurt that he wouldn't even write to him. It was only then that Andy started sequestering himself in his room, keeping the "real world" out. Years later, his parents told him the truth, but by then the damage had already been done. The idea that death itself could be manipulated in such a fashion was never lost on him. After all, didn't Andy's parents fake that the grandfather was still alive by not telling Andy the truth? It was here where I believe Andy would develop the concept of "bending reality" to suit his needs. If his parents could fake his grandfather's not dying, Andy would just fake himself dying. I'm no Sherlock Holmes, but if there was ever an example of "deductive reasoning," this is it. Kaufman's coming back. I'd stake my reputation on it.

*   *   *

Andy had literally a laundry list of so-called "mental disorders" as diagnosed by three leading psychiatrists.* I hesitate to categorize these psychological conditions as "disorders" because in Andy's case he successfully integrated them into his act and publicity campaigns, reaping the benefits of fame and fortune by doing so. These "disorders" would become the very clay he used to mold his sculptures of performance art, where he himself would be both sculptor and sculpture. There are many who believe that he may have been our first performance artist. It is comforting to know that today he is recognized as an important artist whose influence has been felt worldwide.

1. Dissociative identity disorder, formerly referred to as multiple personality disorder

   "The essential feature of this disorder is the presence of two or more distinct identities or personality states. Each personality state may be experienced as if it has a distinct personal history, self image, and identity, including a separate name."

   The obvious example would be his alter-ego, lounge singer Tony Clifton. Clifton had his own friends, wardrobe, even car. Whereas Andy was a strict vegetarian health nut, nonsmoker, and teetotaler, Clifton consumed steaks (rare), chain smoked, and gulped down Jack Daniel's as if there was no tomorrow.

2. Obsessive-compulsive disorder
   His classic routines rarely varied. Watch his Foreign-Man-Becomes-Elvis routine, a beat-for-beat pattern, every utterance and gesture duplicated time and time again with

---

* All quoted materials that follow were found in the *Diagnostic and Statistical Manual of Mental Disorders*, 5th edition.

unerring precision. His compulsive washing of his hands, often dozens of times a day. He was always compelled to say goodbye to a hotel room in which he had stayed every time he checked out. After exiting his car and locking it, he walked around it exactly three times to make sure the doors were in fact locked. On visiting his home you were required to remove your shoes. Andy carefully washed his silverware at restaurants before using it. Into his water glass he dunked each implement one at a time, then took it out and dried it with his napkin. He made sure that no clothing, with the exception of night clothing, ever came in contact with his bedding. One of his oddest eccentricities related to air travel. Whenever Andy boarded a plane, he did so with his right foot first, and as his traveling companion you were required to follow suit. If you were walking down the street with him and passed a light pole or some other hazard, it was mandatory you both did so on the same side. If you split up and walked on either side, he'd make you return so you could both run through it again and get it right.

Lynne

We had discussions about splitting up and walking around something. If it wasn't practical to go back and correct it, saying, "Bread and butter" would suffice to negate the bad luck. When in New York, we had to come to the agreement that people didn't count; it's impossible to walk in New York and not be separated by people. I was content with this, but Andy later admitted that he still said, "Bread and butter" silently whenever someone walked between us! Another one of his obsessions was when he put the key in the lock to open his front door. When we were first together, I couldn't help but notice that he had to wiggle his front door key a lot to get the door open. I told him he could easily get that fixed, but then he admitted that what he was doing was wiggling the key a certain number of times before he opened the door. If I said something that distracted him, he had to start all over. I learned to keep my mouth shut while he was unlocking the door! Same with meditating: his meditation program should have lasted about an hour but if he fell asleep during meditation (which he often did) he would start over and sometimes his meditation could take hours. And this was twice a day!

3. Sexual masochism

> "Involves the act (real, not simulated) of being humiliated, beaten, bound, or otherwise made to suffer. Some males with sexual masochism also have sexual sadism. Masochistic sexual fantasies are likely to have been present in childhood. Sexual masochism is usually chronic, and the person tends to repeat the same masochistic act."

I believe Andy's first encounter with masochism in the form of "humiliation" was when he believed his beloved grandfather Papu had walked out on him. He would learn to repeat, if not welcome, this humiliation throughout his entire life both onstage and off.

4. Sexual sadism

> "Involves acts in which the individual derives sexual excitement from the psychological or physical suffering (including humiliation) of the victim. In such cases the sadistic fantasies usually involve having complete control over the victim."

This would account for Andy's sexual mate having to remain totally immobile during the sex act, as Lynne and others attest.

Lynne

He said that it was because it reminded him of his first sexual encounter, which was with a Jayne Mansfield-shaped hot-water bottle when he was a kid. He would lie on top of the bottle and rub it until he came to climax. Dr. Zmudee recounted this phenomenon in his book, Andy Kaufman Revealed! *"Frottage." But even if that were the reason, why hang on so obsessively to such an impulse? And he would tell me (and any other woman) that he wanted me to "play dead" while we had sex. Just like the doll.*

Forcing an audience to sit perfectly still while he read *The Great Gatsby* in its entirety, along with his wrestling positions, which would "immobilize" his opponent, are two key examples of this behavior.

5. Anti-social personality disorder

"The essential features of this disorder include not liking rules, hating authority, and getting what one wants by manipulating others."

While the trade of your average comedian is to point out the idiosyncrasies and quirks of society, Kaufman delves deeper into these disorders not often associated with light-hearted comedic fodder. It's dark, it's different, it's punk, it's Kaufmanesque, and soon it would not be tolerated in a medium such as television, which was designed to sedate, not agitate. Ebersol/Michaels must take full responsibility for bringing the "monster" into the laboratory (SNL) and giving him life (exposure on national TV). When the creature ultimately became uncontrollable and dangerous, some would say Ebersol had the good sense to pull the plug and try to warn the villagers, but not before the "monster" had ravaged the countryside.

*   *   *

What I know of Andy I saw with my own two eyes from 1974 to 1984. Ten years. Still, I am intrigued when I hear about the Andy that people knew before that time. Remember, when I met him, although he wasn't a television star yet, he was already a success-ful cabaret act in New York City. Anyone who had his pulse on the NYC club scene knew Andy was a force to be reckoned with. And he knew it too. He was experiencing success for the first time in his adult life.

But I'm told by friends of his that just a few years earlier, around 1969, he was still terribly shy and introverted. Prudence Farrow (made famous by the Beatles song "Dear Prudence," and Mia's sister) was one of his TM instructors in Cambridge at the time. She said he would get tongue-tied when he tried to speak to her. Painfully shy. She and other friends of his worried terribly about him, realizing he had no skills whatsoever and that they couldn't see him working at any kind of job. Most of them are still in shock to this day that he became as successful as he did, as they all feared he actually would have become a street nut. Of course he believed that it was the TM that gave him the confidence to perform in front of people, and he kept it up religiously even after the movement gave him the boot.

CHAPTER 5

Andy's Secret

"Andy came into my office the day that John Belushi died and he was very upset. He said, 'John Belushi is pulling my stunt, faking his death.' He actually believed for a while that Belushi had done it. He spoke to me numerous times about faking his death. 'Could you imagine how this is going to blow everyone's mind?' He cherished making headlines, the bigger the better. And nothing will be bigger than his return."

— George Shapiro

Ring …

B: Andy, it's Bob. So who else did you tell?

A: Tell about what?

B: You know what I'm talking about.

A: No one.

B: Are you sure?

A: Maybe Mimi Lambert.

B: Maybe?

A: OK, I did. I told Mimi.

B: Who's Mimi Lambert?

A: You remember Mimi. She's the girl I wrestled on SNL.

B: Oh, yeah. She was hot. What did you tell her? [Silence.] Andy?

A: I told her I was going to fake my death by making people believe I had terminal cancer.

B: Jesus!

A: I know. I shouldn't have done it.

B: Damn right you shouldn't have done it! If you keep telling people, you might as well call the whole thing off. It might even be too late already.

A: Don't worry. It will all work out in the long run.

B: What did she say?

A: She thought it was disgusting and if I ever brought it up again, she'd never talk to me.

B: That's why you can't tell people about it. Some people really get wigged out when you start fucking with death. It's so terrifying to them that they think it's taboo to even joke about it.

A: I know. That's why I like the Mexicans. They throw big parties for the dead the day after Halloween.

B: Yeah. Day of the Dead. November 1. They play music, dance on the graves, eat tamales, drink tequila, even fuck right on the graves!

A: When I was a teenager, me and my friends used to jump the fence of the cemetery at night and drink till dawn.

B: I can't picture you drinking.

A: I was a total drunk. Drank every day for two years straight. Dropped LSD. Smoked weed. I enjoyed it. Had a good time with my friends. But then when I got into TM, I stopped it cold.

B: Do you ever miss it?

A: No. Today I just focus on my career and meditate. But back then I was as close as one can get to being a wino. It was pretty scary.

B: Jesus, just imagine—you could have ended up on a street corner reading *The Great Gatsby* for spare change.

A: If I hadn't found TM, that's exactly what I'd be doing. But I'd be playing the congas instead. I don't think reading *Gatsby* would have brought in too much.

B: So are you admitting George is right?

A: He is right, but that doesn't mean I'm going to stop reading it.

B: That's the spirit!

*   *   *

I remember the first time I heard the rumors. A hooker at Joe Conforte's Mustang Ranch told me. I had "dated" her a few times. She was a petite little redhead with a killer bod. Kaufman never chose her, she said, because, "He likes the bigger, muscular girls that were better equipped for wrestling. It fulfilled his fantasy of being with a man." "Fantasy of being with a man?" I said and laughed heartily. She said, "You mean you don't know?" "Know what?" I asked. "He's gay," she said. "Don't be ridiculous. Andy Kaufman gay? Very funny." The redhead turned quite serious and said, "You really don't know, do you?" I said, "Andy's not gay. Jesus Christ, he and I have been coming to the Ranch here for years. He's been having sex with more girls than I do. What the hell would a gay guy be coming here for?" She said, "He goes both ways. Some guys who come here do. Haven't you heard of bisexuality?" "Of course I have. Besides, how would you know?" I asked. "You admitted you never slept with him." "I haven't," she said, "but all us girls talk. We compare notes all the time. He's an ass bandit alright, even pays extra for it. Always wants the girls to lay flat on their stomachs and not move, so he doesn't see their breasts or vaginas that way. From the back they appear as a young boy." The conversation, even though I didn't believe her, was making me pretty uncomfortable. "Can we change the subject?" I asked. "Sorry, I didn't mean to freak you out." I said, "You're not freaking me out 'cause I don't believe you." She didn't mention another word after that, sensing not only that she did freak me out, but also that she'd killed the possibility of my choosing her to go back to.

I had a few more drinks at the bar as I waited for Andy to come out of one of the bedrooms. When he emerged, I was pretty smashed. The girl on his arm was bigger than he was and not particularly attractive or feminine for that matter, just the type the redhead had described. Still, I couldn't get my head around what she had told me. I guess I didn't want to.

As we jumped into the car and drove back toward Reno, I was quieter than usual. In a happy-go-lucky voice, Andy said, "Well, aren't you going to ask me?" I became alarmed, but didn't show it. "Ask you what?" I said, not sure where he was going with this. "Ask me how she was, of course," something we always asked each other afterward. "Oh, yeah, of course. So how was she?" He smiled and in the Clifton voice said, "She was good, but I was better." We both laughed. I thought to myself, "That redhead is full of shit." I thought of telling Andy what she said, because I really didn't believe it, but for some unknown reason didn't. It was just too uncomfortable a subject even to bring up, and over the next couple of years, it disappeared completely from my psyche. Andy Kaufman gay? Give me a break.

It wasn't until years later that Lynne confirmed Andy's little secret.

* * *

Lynne

This "secret" of Andy's seems so last week in this day and age. The world has changed so much, but when Andy was alive his "secret" would have been a big deal and could have damaged his career even more than he already had. I don't know that he was in fact worried about his career, but he certainly didn't want his parents to know. In fact, his bisexuality would be so humdrum today that I considered not even mentioning it, but Bob and I agreed that we would be completely honest in this book, since it is most likely the last book we will write about Andy.

So what made me first start wondering if maybe Andy was bisexual? It started creeping into my mind when we were living together in San Francisco and he insisted that I find an apartment in the Castro district, which as everyone knows is one of the most famous gay districts in the world. He said it was because there was a Mrs. Fields cookie store there. This was a perfectly believable reason because in Andy's world, cookies and chocolate cake were king. He also said he wanted to be near Little Orphan Andy's and Sparky's, two twenty-four-hour restaurants that we frequented in the wee hours. It only dawned on me later to wonder how the heck he knew so much about the Castro in the first place.

So I found an apartment on Collingwood Street at the top of Castro Hill. Andy used to go down the hill every day to Mrs. Fields to get his chocolate chip cookie fix. It didn't occur to me at the time that he was going down there for anything else.

Now that we were together for long stretches of time, I began to wonder where he disappeared to for hours at a time. He said he was at a coffee shop writing his book. This too was totally believable, but questions kept popping up in my mind and I started to put two and two together.

Like the hooker told Bob, Andy was extremely sexually attracted to tall, muscular women. Girls who pumped iron were particularly arousing to him. It didn't matter to him what they looked like. He gave me an example of this. He told me that he tried to get Sandra Bernhard to wrestle him because he found her sexually attractive because she was "more like a man than a woman." (Sorry, Sandra!) He was very disappointed that she wanted nothing to do with him. (Back then, he probably didn't know that she herself was gay.) This proclivity for "mannish" bodies got me wondering about his sexual preferences; I started to wonder if perhaps Andy was gay but couldn't face it or admit it to himself. I didn't say anything to him initially because I didn't really care. But I did mention it to Bob, who I think was a little homophobic about it and just didn't want to discuss it.

So why did he get so aroused when he wrestled women? Was it because he couldn't wrestle men? I've since looked closely at the match where Andy was given the pile driver by Jerry Lawler, and yep, he is indeed "pitching a tent" as he gets carried off on the stretcher!

When he had sex with women, he wanted them to "play dead." He didn't want any moaning or physical involvement from them. He just wanted them to lie there while he humped away. I know for a fact that it wasn't just me because I asked him if it was that way with every woman he slept with and he confirmed it. Bob told me that the hookers he talked to said the same thing.

Years after Andy "died," a gay friend in San Francisco said that everyone knew Andy died of AIDS because they saw him in the Castro district constantly.

Anyway, I finally just point-blank asked him if he was gay. He looked at me for a long time as he was formulating his answer, probably trying to decide if he wanted to tell me. He finally lowered his head and said in a small voice, "Yeah." And I just laughed and said, "Andy, I don't care a bit! I already know that you have sex with other women, why should men bother me?" And we both started laughing. I asked if Bob knew, and Andy said, "NO!" He hadn't told Bob, he didn't know how he would react. I said I thought he should come clean, and he said he would think about it. It wasn't until we were in the Philippines that he finally told Bob the truth, but by then I had already discussed it with Bob.

* * *

Lynne prepared me that Andy was going to tell me he was gay, although he didn't know that I already knew at the time. He was propped up in bed at the hotel he was staying in, in Baguio City in the Philippines. Lynne held his hand and said to me, "Dr. Zmudee—Andy has something to tell you." I knew what was coming and could see he was quite conflicted about telling me. So I made it easy on him and said, "Andy, if it's about you being gay … I've known for years." He was so relieved when I said that. "You did?" "Of course," I said. "You couldn't have idolized Fabian for all those years because of his singing voice!" He laughed and then said, "No, he really did have a good voice!" And that was it. Ten years of hiding in the closet with me was over in just twenty seconds. Such a burden was immediately taken off his shoulders. He soon got out of bed and we all went down to the hotel's restaurant to have a good meal. We never mentioned it again, although he told Lynne he didn't want his parents to know, and we shouldn't tell anybody until both of them had passed away. His mother died soon after Andy did, but his dad, a tough old coot who was awarded three Purple Hearts, lived to be ninety and died on July 25, 2013. Lynne and I honored Andy's wishes.

I don't know if Andy's brother and sister will be shocked by this revelation or not. For all Lynne and I know, they might have known all these years. What may be shocking to them is the suggestion that he might have died of AIDS, although I'm sure they, like myself, haven't escaped the rumors that have persisted for years. We are no longer living in the dark ages of this disease. If he had possibly contracted it from a man, as Lynne suggested, so be it. He just as easily could have picked it up from one of the countless prostitutes he had sex with, if that makes it more palatable for the family. And for all I know, the family may already know this too. Nobody is talking and that is unfortunate. Perhaps this book will get a dialogue going between Lynne, Michael, Carol, and me. I could only hope. It's time for all the skeletons to come out of the closet.

*   *   *

Over the years, my friends and I would hold occasional séances in hopes of getting in contact with Andy in case he had crossed over to the other side. We held these usually on the anniversary of his supposed death, May 16. Even though initially I did it for fun (knowing Andy was still alive), I still would bring in top respected psychics and invite some of my celebrity friends to attend. I remember one year we held the séance upstairs in the "Belly Room" of Mitzi Shore's The Comedy Store. The place is haunted. It's the real thing. In fact, some of Mitzi Shore's staff simply refuses to go up there when the club's closed.

On one particular May 16, I brought in a top psychic and invited Bobcat Goldthwait, Bob Saget, Andy Dick, Sally Kirkland, and other friends to attend a midnight séance. It wasn't long into the séance when the lights in the ninety-seat showroom started to blink on and off. Contact was made, but not with Andy. Instead it was the spirit of a woman. The medium said she was a showgirl who used to work in the club as a dancer back in the '40s when the club was called "Ciro's," a very popular show room where big stars such as Martin and Lewis, Sophie Tucker, Jimmy Durante, and the like used to perform. It was Mafia-owned back then, and this girl got knocked up by a married celebrity patron and had a botched illegal abortion performed on her in the "Belly Room" itself, where she died.

Now I'm usually skeptical about such things. The psychic I brought that evening knew nothing about the history of the room. Neither did I at the time and took what the psychic said with a grain of salt.

But here's where things get weird. Months after the séance, I was talking to the owner, Mitzi Shore. She asked how the séance went. Half jokingly, I started to tell her about what the psychic had said about this woman. Mitzi stopped me and said the psychic was good, and then she continued to tell me the whole story, which matched just what the psychic had said. I couldn't believe my ears.

Since then, I've held other séances with other psychics and not one has been able to make contact with Andy. Why? The answer is obvious: he's not dead.

Over the years Andy would give me and others that knew him little signs here and there that he was listening and wanted us to know. Something innocent enough such as thinking about him and the next thing you know, the song "Man on the Moon" would come on the radio. Granted, some would say that's a mere coincidence, but if you've experienced it like I have countless times, just when you were thinking about him, you couldn't help but feel something else was at play. And then, of course, there would be those times when it would be impossible to dismiss it as mere coincidence, such as the *Leprechaun 2* episode.

It all started innocently enough on one particular occasion. I, along with George Shapiro and Howard West, had a very important "pitch" meeting with an executive at NBC named Rick Ludwin. We wanted to sell him *A Comedy Salute to Andy Kaufman,* a one-hour retrospective of Andy's work. This was ten years after Andy's supposed death and a real long shot at a possible sale.

Now the night before an important pitch, I'm usually pretty anxious and wound up and have a tendency toward insomnia. Over the years, to combat it, I've come up with a solution that seems to work. I'll go to the video store and pick up two or three bad movies—real stinkers, that I'll plop into my VCR. And I'll have such a hard time watching that they'll put me to sleep. On this occasion, one of the turkeys that I rented was called *Leprechaun 2.* Halfway through it, I was out cold, when my own loud snore woke me up. I opened my weary eyes to the TV screen and there it was: an image appeared as clear as day. It read, "Andy Kaufman died for our sins" and then it disappeared. What had just happened? Adrenaline rushed through my body trying to make sense of what I'd just seen on the screen. I rubbed my eyes. I was now wide awake. I had to be hallucinating, but rewound the tape a minute or two back. Sure enough, the image was there once again: "Andy Kaufman died for our sins." It was graffiti on a public bathroom wall in a scene. Now I ask you, what are the odds of your going in to pitch an Andy Kaufman special the next morning, your renting a B-horror film to help you fall asleep, which you do, and it just so happens that you wake up just at the precise moment that that graffiti wall appears? Literally, if I had woken up five or six seconds later, I would have missed it.

The next morning, right before the pitch, I told George about it. He said, "It's a sign from Andy from the other side. It means they're going to buy the special." George was right. They did. That year it was actually nominated for an Emmy.

A few years later, after my first book, *Andy Kaufman Revealed!*, came out, I received a letter from the director of *Leprechaun 2* telling me how he enjoyed the read. I called him up and told him my "Andy died for our sins" story. At first he didn't know what the hell I was talking about, but then remembered. "Oh, yeah," he said. "I remember that scene. We were shooting in a public bathroom. To me, the place looked too pristine. I grabbed a few magic markers and started to graffiti up the stalls, not even giving much thought to what I was writing. I quickly wrote, 'Andy Kaufman died for our sins.' I don't know why. I never wrote that before or after."

Like I said before, George believed it was Andy signaling us from the other side. He was wrong. It wasn't Andy signaling from the other side, but signaling us from *this* side. Here's how it was explained to me by experts in the field of parapsychology and Transcendental Meditation. Since Andy was advanced in TM and practiced it twice a day every day, he was able in his alpha stage to experience OBE (out-of-body experience), or what is commonly referred to in the field as "traveling clairvoyance"—i.e., while meditating, he could send himself just about anywhere, such as influencing the director to write, "Andy Kaufman died for our sins," and years later causing me to wake up just at the right moment to read it.

I had been with him once before when he was OBE-ing. We were on a flight from Chicago to Indiana aboard a small Piper Cub, just Andy, the pilot, and me, when we got caught up in a massive storm. The tiny plane was being pitched around so violently that the pilot gave up the controls, completely lost his composure, and began to pray, convinced we were going to crash. I was on the verge of losing it myself until I looked across at Andy, who was deep in meditation with a pleasant, plaintive smile on his face, totally oblivious to the certain death around us. I tried shaking him awake to no avail. I even lifted one of his eyelids and saw his eye pulsating back and forth in R.E.M. (rapid eye movement). He wasn't there! GONE! Out of nowhere, the storm suddenly dissipated, and we landed safely. Andy came back around and told us he was able to stop the thunderstorm by transporting himself under a waterfall in Paraguay and conversing with a Hindu water goddess. The pilot believed him and kept hugging and thanking him for saving his life. I wouldn't have believed it if I didn't see it with my eyes either. Later, I learned from sources within the TM movement that Andy had learned the technique of "astral projection" from the maharishi himself.

*   *   *

Serial killer/cannibal Jeffrey Dahmer is having dinner with his mother at his apartment. She says, "Jeffrey, I don't like your friends." Jeffrey replies, "So try the potatoes."

Family is the last to know what is really going on in another family member's head. The Kaufmans were no exception. They knew nothing of Andy. Still don't. They had compartmentalized him as an eight-year-old his whole life and never wanted him to grow up. Andy, in turn, fed into the sham. It was a lot easier for him to endure family events that way. I attended a few family affairs, such as Seders. So did Lynne. To us, everybody would be talking to him in baby talk. They had been doing it for so long I'm not even sure if they themselves were aware of it. As he grew older, he eventually moved to the West Coast. Still, when they got together, he'd immediately revert to the baby talk. It is this family dysfunction of being stuck in a childhood time warp that I feel has stunted their appreciation of his adult work. Anything outside of his childlike Mighty Mouse and Cow Goes Moo bits is met with scorn and condemnation from members of the clan.

Even now, the family, in a futile attempt, tries to restrict the material they don't personally approve of from ever being seen. Take the movie. If it wasn't going to deal primarily with his child-hood, they wanted nothing to do with it. They just couldn't bring themselves to accept that Andy had grown up, because growing up meant leaving home and leaving them. So if they couldn't be a part of it, their main mission in life would be to attack it, which they did.

Michael Kaufman would be the first one to say his tastes are quite conservative. So are his sister Carol's. That's why, as the curators of Andy's estate, Michael and Carol have the responsibility to look beyond their likes and dislikes and think of Andy's. They should not try to rewrite his legacy. The best they can do is simply step aside and let the public decide what it wants to see. I was Andy's writer for ten years. Nobody—and I mean *nobody*—knew his wishes better than I did.

If this sounds arrogant, so be it. If there's one thing we can all learn from Andy, it's "don't hide your light under a shovel." For years I was content to remain in the shadows. When I finally came out in *Andy Kaufman Revealed!* and stated, "I was his writer," I was met with some skepticism. After all, Andy was a "madman." How could a madman "have a writer"?

Here's Andy from an April 1980 interview with the men's magazine *Oui:*

> KAUFMAN: Yeah. *The Tony Clifton Story.* They're trying to get him [Tony] for it, and I'm writing it.
>
> OUI: Quite remarkable. By the way, do you write all your own material?
>
> KAUFMAN: Well, I do have a writing partner, Bob Zmuda. I met him around 1973, at the Improv in New York. We used to exchange ideas. I finally said, "You know, you're the only guy I know who could write for me."

So take notice, any "revisionists" out there.

Lynne came in later in the game, but is respected nonetheless. Her documentary *I'm from Hollywood* is brilliant. Andy trusted her artistic insights. Both she and I have worked tirelessly to "keep him out there." We don't do what we do for money. We do it as a labor of love.

*   *   *

Andy, you've got to come back, if for no other reason than to clear things up between Lynne and your brother and sister. I don't get it. Lynne, as you know, is one of the sweetest people in the world. So are Michael and Carol, but they're going at it with Lynne like the Hatfields and McCoys.

It's been building for years. They think Lynne ripped off a lot of your stuff.

*   *   *

Lynne

When Andy died, if indeed he really did, whatever of his possessions were not in our Pacific Palisades house or San Francisco apartment were in storage. He had put almost all of his belongings in storage after moving out of his Laurel Canyon house. When Taxi was canceled, Andy no longer felt the need to live in Los Angeles; that's when we got the apartment in San Francisco. After he was gone, his dad Stanley hired Andy's friend and former secretary Linda Mitchell to get rid of all the "junk." I believe that Linda sent some things to the Kaufmans, kept a few things for herself, and sent the rest of Andy's belongings to my mom's house in San Fernando, where I temporarily stored them in her garage. I talked to Stanley about it; Andy's record collection, his personal papers, etc.; and he said, "Keep it all." Michael Kaufman made a trip to my mom's house at one point to see if he wanted anything. He took a few things and that was that. I have been caring for Andy's belongings since 1984, moving them from home to home, paying thousands of dollars in storage fees. And now Michael is accusing me of stealing these things? He could have taken everything back in 1984, but I guess it was just too much trouble. But now thirty years later he is suddenly calling me a thief when he always knew I had Andy's belongings? That hurts.

Before Andy died, he made me promise to get all of his work out into the world so that his work would not be forgotten. He made me swear this in front of George Shapiro and my friend Wave Geber. He told them they were witnesses and he made George promise to help me. George promised that he would. So, first I finished I'm from Hollywood *according to Andy's wishes and George helped with that in that he set up the interviews with Robin Williams, Marilu Henner, and Tony Danza. He also was trying to help me sell it but my investors were not very savvy and they drove him crazy. So he did help with* Hollywood. *But after that was finished, I got ready to dive into getting the rest of his work out as I promised, and called George to make a plan. George said something like, "What? No, I promised to help with* I'm from Hollywood, *nothing else." In other words, "Fergit-aboutit baby! Get out of Hollywood and let the big boys take over."*

*   *   *

Andy, Lynne said after you supposedly died that Stanley wanted to get rid of everything and told her she could have it all. Now thirty years later your career has improved and your memorabilia is worth something, and your family wants it all back.

Remember that *Grandmother* album you always wanted to do? Lynne "got it out there" like you wanted. Your dad went berserk. At first he thought I did it and started bitching about me. When they found out it was Lynne, they went bonkers! Got lawyers after her and everything.

*   *   *

Lynne

*One of the things Andy very dearly wanted to do was to make
an album out of the mini-cassette recordings he had made. In the
late '70s, after hearing Bob's stories about Norman Wexler tape
recording everything he did, Andy decided he would do that too.
He carried a mini-cassette recorder everywhere and recorded
everything and everyone. His grandma, his girlfriends, strangers on the street. He would create situations in public so that he
could capture the reaction on tape. He admired an album that
Steve Allen had put out in the '60s called* Funny Fone Calls
*and wanted to do something similar with his tapes. I had duti-
fully carried the tapes around for twenty-five years and wasn't
able to drum up any interest until, in 2008, I made a book deal
with Process Media to release* Dear Andy Kaufman, I Hate
Your Guts, *a compilation of hate mail that Andy received from
women after challenging them to wrestle on* Saturday Night
Live. *My publisher, Jodi Wille, immediately saw the potential
of Andy's tapes and hooked me up with Drag City Records, a
small independent label out of Chicago. I was so happy because
finally I was able to fulfill Andy's dream of making an album
out of the tapes! But right before the album was to come out, on
the release date, as a matter of fact, I got a threatening letter
from the Kaufmans via a lawyer telling Drag City and me to
cease and desist! I couldn't believe it. Until that moment, I had
believed that the Kaufmans and I were completely on the same
page with the same goal: to get Andy's work out into the world.
That's what Andy wanted and what I've always worked toward.
I mean, there's no money in this, come on. It's a labor of love.
But here was this letter. I tried to call Michael to talk about
it, but in response got an even nastier letter from his lawyer.
Wow. Luckily, Drag City had already produced the album, so
I just walked away from the deal and gave it to the Kaufmans.
All that mattered was getting the album out. But they weren't*

through yet. After that I started getting threatening letters about Andy's belongings! The belongings that Stanley Kaufman had given to me and that I had cared for all these years. These belongings had recently been the core of a New York gallery show called On Creating Reality *by Andy Kaufman. This was a huge, prestigious show that cemented Andy's contributions to performance art and television. Bob even insisted that Michael Kaufman be involved. I thought that the Kaufmans would be thrilled that, through Bob and me, this recognition of Andy as an important presence in art and performance was happening. Instead I found out later that they were livid! What the hell? I am truly baffled by their behavior.*

*　　*　　*

I told Lynne you're coming back and will straighten everything out. She thinks I've lost my mind, of course. In retrospect, next time you do something like this, leave a will. Then it will be clear what your wishes are. I'll tell you one thing, I never used to think about having a will until I witnessed this crap. I know you never gave much thought to the "almighty dollar," so it's going to be interesting to see if your philosophy has changed with age. When you're young, you feel infallible, but the older people get, the more they run scared.

Oh, get this—remember the Moonlight Brothel in Carson, Nevada? Like how can you forget! Anyway, remember that big guy named Dennis? He once put up one hundred dollars if one of the girls could pin your shoulders—and then when the girl couldn't do it, he gave her the money anyway? Well, guess what—he now owns the place. It's now called Dennis Hof's World Famous Bunny Ranch. You've seen it on HBO, if you have HBO. It's a series called *Cathouse.* He's been so successful in the world's oldest profession that he now owns seven brothels altogether. Well, he and I are buddies. He's going to be there when you return with a half dozen of his top girls and here's what he's offered to do because he's such a big fan of yours: Any customer who buys a ticket to see you, all he has to do is show up at Dennis's brothel the next day and his ticket stub will be good for one free hooker. I'm not joking. He personally is going to pay for the hookers out of his own pocket. If 400 people show up from the night before, so be it. The hookers are on him!

So screw you if you don't show up! Some people are going to buy a ticket just to get the free hooker. Like Dennis says, "There's no business like ho-business!" Of course, you're going to have to partake yourself the next day. He's got more than a few that will knock your socks off. Some real big ugly ones too, the kind that you like.

Speaking of hookers, remember the time we were playing Harrah's in Reno for a week's run? Lisa Hartman was your opening act. It was the first time we went to Joe Conforte's Mustang Ranch, and you made a bet that you would screw all forty-two girls before you left town and *did*! Remember the last day there were like six girls remaining and you said, "My penis feels like it has been through a meat grinder," but you pulled it off, all forty-two. Those were the good old days. Well, soon they'll be back, and this time you'll have to break your old record.

What a show! Free hookers! Wrestling! I'm also going to reach out to R.E.M. to see if I can get them to perform that evening. They split up, you know, but I think I can get them together again for such a once-in-a-lifetime occasion. Maybe that's how we do it—they close the show by playing "Man on the Moon"—three-quarters of the way through the song is when you make your grand appearance! Think about it. How spectacular would that be?

*   *   *

If Andy Kaufman was strange, sex made him normal. The stranger Andy got, the more sex he needed to bring him back to earth. The average male might go to a brothel and have a girl or even two per visit. Andy would have six to eight during the same time period. Even hard-core prostitutes who have worked the Ranch for years would say they never saw anything like it. In a pretentious world, Andy craved the unpretentiousness that sex with hookers provided, as it is the only realm of primordial adventure still left to most of us. He couldn't get enough of it, and the more he got the more he wanted. When the pressure of show business got to be too much, he'd head to the Ranch to "decompress." The girls loved him and found it strange that he displayed no airs of celebrity whatsoever. He seldom talked about himself and was truly more interested in who they were. He developed relationships that would last a lifetime with many of them even after their sexual relations had ended. He flew more than a half dozen out at his own expense to learn TM from instructor and friend Prudence Farrow. One would even knit him sweaters. He never looked down at what they were doing. If anything, he looked up to them as "sexual healers." He didn't "fuck" them, he "made love" to them, and as women they knew the difference. As Norman Mailer once said, if a prostitute can't fall in love with her client, what chance has she? And many of them truly fell in love with Andy. Prostitutes became one of the great joys of his life. He didn't hide the fact that he was into it and believed it should be legal in every state of the Union. It made him happy, so much so that even his parents learned to accept it as a healthy social activity of his. His mother cheerfully referred to it as "Andy going off to camp." It was the perfect situation for him, relationship-wise. He could have companionship any time he wanted it. Frequently he'd fly a girl out to be with him for a few days or even a week or so and then when it was time to get back to work, she just as quickly was out of his hair. What was it Charlie Sheen said—"I don't pay a prostitute for sex. I pay her to leave." That's why all of his friends were flabbergasted when Lynne came on the scene. She was so different from any "civilian" girl he had ever dated before. For one thing, she was an artist in her own right, well adjusted, attractive, and had no problem with his sexual romps whatsoever, just as long as he came home to her at night. Prudence Farrow, a close confidante of Andy's, told me she was so happy when he met Lynne for she felt for the first time in all the years she'd known him that he'd finally met somebody he was serious about. He told her he'd "met his soul mate." Had he not faked his death, there is no doubt in my mind that he would have married her. That is why I'm till this very day suspicious of what she knows or doesn't about his disappearance. She's old-school wrestling code of silence—"loose lips sink ships"—and since I adhere to the same code, I would never ask her what she knows or doesn't. Besides, she wouldn't tell me anyway.

$$* \quad * \quad *$$

There is a scene in *Man on the Moon* where Andy is moving into a new house with Lynne when the phone rings. He puts a moving box down and answers. It's George Shapiro calling with some bad news. We know it's bad news because there's sad music playing on the film score, plus George sounds distraught. He tells Andy that *Taxi* has just been canceled. I'm sure the filmmakers would have loved to see Andy saddened by the news, but on the set that day, thank God, Lynne and I were present. When we became aware of where Scott and Larry were going with this, we threw down our gauntlet and said, "Enough, already." If anything, Andy was overjoyed when *Taxi* was canceled. We know this because Lynne was with him when the real call came in. He was just about doing cartwheels. Of course, the screenwriters who are trying to con-struct a story line are using the firing of Andy from SNL and now the cancellation of *Taxi* as a device to lead him spiraling down into getting depressed and sick. Sorry, Scott and Larry, that story structure might have worked for *Jim Thorpe—All-American* and hundreds of other similar films, but Lynne and I weren't going to sit idly by while Hollywood tampered with Andy's essence. Switch a few scenes around here and there and we'll look the other way, but not when it comes to our boy's essence. Never. Not on our watch.

*   *   *

Lynne

True, Andy was ecstatic when Taxi *was canceled. It was like he'd been freed from prison. He immediately moved out of his rented Laurel Canyon house, put his belongings in storage, and turned his attention seriously toward becoming a professional wrestler and getting his revenge on Jerry Lawler. He knew this was his true calling!*

So of course we sat down with Andy/Jim and expressed our concern. Jim wanted to be as accurate as humanly possible about what really came down and truly valued all insights from us. After all, Lynne and I didn't spend eighty days with him to bask in "the glory of all things Jim." There are enough assholes in Hollywood to do that. He knew when it came to the truth about Andy, Lynne and I weren't messing around. So Jim played the scene totally indifferent to George's phone call—not saddened in the least. I'm sure in editing Milos was looking for the take where Jim was injured by the news. Sorry, Milos, it never existed. Oh, yeah, one other thing, also in that scene: He reaches up and feels a boil on his neck. We are to believe it's the start of the cancer. Sorry, guys, it was just a boil on his neck. As for Carnegie Hall being his swan song after he learns he has cancer, wrong again. Carnegie Hall took place nearly six years *before* his supposed death.

*   *   *

Ring …

B: Hello?

A: Hey, Bob, it's Andy.

B: What's up?

A: I went to Madame Tussauds today on Hollywood Boulevard.

B: What did you think?

A: I think I can hire somebody to do a wax figure of myself, put it in a coffin, and people will think it's me. I bet Ken Chase can do it. He made those molds of you and my face for Clifton.

B: Yeah, but I don't know if he works in wax. Besides, how would you get him or somebody like him to swear to secrecy?

A: A portion of the money up front and increments every year people think I'm dead.

B: That could be a lot of money, Andy.

A: I've got a lot of money. You know I don't spend it. What do you think?

B: Like I said before, you got to keep me out of it. What I don't know can't hurt you. Plausible denial.

A: What if the police questioned you?

B: How many times have I played Tony on Letterman, Merv, and everybody thought it was you? I didn't even tell my own mother. Wrestler's code! I'm no rat.

CHAPTER 6

Andy at SNL

S o let me get this straight, Zmuda. Are you telling us that you and Andy purposely plotted to destroy his successful commercial career?

Now you're getting it, Sparky!

But why would anyone want to do that?

You know, over the years, I've been asking myself that very question. I believe it had to do with the youth rebellion that Andy, I, and the whole country were experiencing at the time. The "turbulent '60s." If I was going to make a film about Kaufman today, I'd focus on the time period that most people overlook entirely, and that is when he was fourteen to seventeen years old. He grows his hair long and runs away from home. He's pretty much a teenage alcoholic, doing every drug imaginable, and hell-bent on not being part of the "system." In his hip pocket he carries a worn copy of Jack Kerouac's *On the Road.* It is at this time the friction between him and his father is at an all-time high. Three thousand miles across the country, I'm experiencing a similar rejection of society, the book in my hip pocket being Abbie Hoffman's *Steal This Book.* When he and I join forces, we "conspire" to overthrow the entertainment industry of the United States of America. It was in our

DNA. It's how society grows. New ideas replacing old. Were we at times arrogant and self-indulgent in that quest? Probably. We were the avant-garde and had to be.

So what were we fighting for? Freedom. Artistic freedom. Freedom from the constraints of commercial entertainment. Freedom from the shackles of the pre-recorded laugh track. (Did you know those people are dead?) Freedom from the tyranny of the punch line. Freedom from the fourth wall. Freedom from cue cards. Freedom from the Not Ready for Prime Time Players. Freedom from the Jewish stand-up industrial complex. Freedom from laughter itself, if need be. It's exciting that today there is a whole new generation who don't even watch TV anymore. It's all Internet now. Thousands of young people around the planet uploading their own homemade videos, creating whole new worlds, new ways of looking at things, no longer being driven by mindless consumption. Exciting times. That's why Kaufman is more relevant today than ever before. He's become a role model for today's disaffected youth that sees no worth in a broken-down economic model that no longer works. Andy revolted against the entire entertainment industry. He's basically the Che Guevara of the Borscht Belt.

*   *   *

Lynne

And there is my argument why Andy couldn't be alive; he wouldn't be able to resist having his own Internet TV show! The Internet was made for Andy; if it had existed in the early '80s, Andy would have had a camera in his house and recorded his every movement. He would have invented reality TV. In 1983, when no one except David Letterman would have him on their shows after all the trouble he had caused, he was very excited about having an all-night cable TV show in San Francisco. He would play all the stuff he liked, and in between, when you cut back to the host of the show (Andy), he would be asleep on a couch and the camera would hold on him for however long the break was.

*   *   *

Actor Paul Giamatti, who played me in the film, was beginning to figure out some of it: "I think Andy was onto the idea that adulation for celebrities can be very close to despising them. There is a really fine line there, and he and Zmuda were playing around with that. The weirdest thing about him was that a lot of his stuff wasn't funny. He was just forcing people's minds to open wider." Chris Rock said, "Andy Kaufman was like Miles Davis." Bob Odenkirk added, "Andy thought everything was a fucking joke, because the bottom line is we're all fools, idiots, and jackasses." As Dana Carvey once said, "All roads lead to Kaufman."

There's always a price paid for "bringing in the new" and Andy was only human. He did at times worry that he might end up a has-been with his pushing of the envelope. Still, he'd rather be true to his art than play it safe doing *Taxi*, which he felt was "somebody else's playground."

*   *   *

Lynne

That was the beauty of Andy's work. If he really did become a "has-been," well, he had already glorified has-beens in his work! So perhaps being a has-been was all part of the act. He also thought he would become a wrestling manager. Now, most Hollywood stars would be appalled at the thought of lowering themselves to the level of professional wrestling, but to Andy, being a wrestling manager would have been the epitome of greatness, the culmination of his career. Fuck movies, fuck Taxi. He didn't care how much money he made, he was in it for the purity of his art. And to have fun, of course.

Could George Shapiro have done more to support Andy's artistry? Perhaps. He tried because he knew Andy was original and at times brilliant. But Shapiro is a Hollywood manager in the traditional sense. It all gets down to making as much money as possible for his client and his agency. He knew Andy was ahead of his time, but George and his partner Howard West lived in the present. I hope that today George takes pride in the many accolades and praise that Andy is receiving. Andy and George both deserve it. George backed his friend and it cost George. After all, it was George who got the phone calls of rage from producers and club owners when Andy got into his "destructive mode." As George said, "I suffered more than Andy, because the backlash came directly to me." In one particular incident, Andy had George book Tony Clifton on *The Dinah Shore Show,* a homogenized effluent of mindless patter and less-than-trivial guests, all contrived to give its target—stultified, mid-life housewives—something to watch in the afternoon. During a cooking segment with Dinah, she said something that set Tony off. Clifton picks up a bowl of freshly whipped egg batter and pours it over her head. Picture the film *Carrie* with the bucket of blood. Bedlam breaks loose. Clifton is once again unceremoniously escorted out of the studio by security. George apologetically sent cases of champagne and flowers to Dinah and the producer of the show for two weeks in a row. It's funny. Nowadays George himself has taken up TM, along with his client Jerry Seinfeld. I guess if you can't beat 'em, join 'em.

*   *   *

Here's an interesting insight that Andy shared with his manager George Shapiro:

> It used to be my playground, George, and now I feel it's somebody else's playground. I need to feel that it's my playground again. And by doing routines like The Great Gatsby and wrestling—even if

nobody likes it—it's necessary to feel it's my playground again. This year has been a very commercial year for me with *Taxi* and everything and that's great commercially. It gets more people out to see my live show. But I've been feeling down artistically. I want to start having integrity in what I do again, or else I'm just like everybody else.

George loved Andy and because of that he wanted him to be happy. So George was torn between a successful commercial career, which Andy hated, and his being true to his artistic standards, which would be a career-killer. George would harken back to the early days of Andy's career. Before reading *The Great Gatsby*, which would clear the room, Andy had been doing another bit that was equally deadly, called appropriately "the Bombing Routine." I think even today if you mention "the Bombing Routine" around George, his blood pressure will start to rise.

"The Bombing Routine" is just as its name implies. Andy would be in his Foreign Man character and start doing terrible impressions, which sounded nothing like the person. How could it? After all, he was speaking in his Foreign Man accent. But he'd go on, impression after impression—Jimmy Carter, Archie Bunker, Ed Sullivan, etc.—each impression worse than the one before. The audience would laugh, but only because it was so bad. Soon Foreign Man would figure it out and say to the audience, "You're not laughing *with* me, but *at* me," and begin to cry uncontrollably. Soon, he would strike his conga on the downbeat of every sob until he created a steady rhythm. The routine would end with an incredible conga solo that would bring audiences to their feet … sometimes. If Andy didn't like the audience or the club manager, or even if he just had a whim, he would never go into the conga beats. He wouldn't strike the conga at all. Instead, he'd just cry. Many a club owner would bring down the curtain on this "Bombing Routine." George would be perplexed as to why Andy would do such a thing. I believe Andy got off from the rejection of being fired and his thumbing his nose at society. It's similar to Miles Davis, who used to turn his back to the audience altogether and face the musicians who were playing behind him.

It's like Pavlov and his young daughter. What Pavlov would do is have a large assortment of delectable foods laid out on the dinner table and then—making sure his daughter was ravenous—he had her sit in front of it, but he wouldn't let her eat. She would sit there just taking it all in, and then he would have the food removed and taken back into the kitchen. He did this over and over again. He believed it "trained" his daughter at an early age to build up a "resistance to disappointment" throughout her entire life.

A similar concept worked on Andy after his grandfather, Papu, stopped coming around. Andy withdrew into himself. Once he came of school age and was forced to be around other kids, he continued to withdraw—very shy and aloof. Kids would be mean to him and taunt him for being such a recluse. But he oddly began to find solace in this loser kind of mentality. It would eventually work for him onstage: his ineptness warranted laughter. The more abuse he could inflict on himself in the Foreign Man character, the more the audiences loved it. Self-denigration works onstage. Before he was famous and recognizable, I actually have watched women in the audience yell at their boyfriends to stop laughing at him. In fact, that became the inside joke. One would bring an unsuspecting friend to The Improv or Catch A Rising Star to basically laugh at this pathetic individual dying on stage. How often have I heard a customer complaining to Budd Friedman (owner of The Improv) that he was an awful person to put this sad man onstage to be ridiculed. Once Dick Ebersol and Lorne Michaels spotted him and put him on national TV, Andy began to be financially rewarded for this behavior. He too would learn a valuable lesson: rejection and hurt became kindred spirits to him. They made him who he was, empowered him like Pavlov's daughter. Eventually he would learn to seek out situations where he would be humiliated and rejected, such as being kicked off *Taxi*, SNL, or the whole entertainment industry, for that matter. It's the same kind of thrill that people who like to cut themselves get. Jeff Conaway said, "I was beating the hell out of him and he loved it." A classic masochist if there ever was one. And now with his new "Dying Routine," he hit pay dirt, for he could witness his own suffering and death just like the Nazarene. But in Andy's case, live to tell about it. Remember the first rule of *Fight Club*? You don't talk about Fight Club. Masochism protected by a code of ethics—the wrestlers' code. Andy Kaufman died for our sins all right, and he is coming back to make sure we haven't forgotten it. Is he going to show? It's impossible for him to stay away. It just "Hurts So Good."

Andy's whole life and act is built around rejections:

His grandfather rejects him.
Kids at school reject him.
Foreign Man is rejected.
Taxi rejected him.
SNL rejected him.
The TM movement rejected him.
Finally, he decides to beat them at their own game, and he rejects *himself* by faking his death.

Rejection, rejection, rejection. It's a theme that would run throughout his entire life. If he no longer exists, he can no longer be rejected. It's spiritual jujitsu. Use your opponent's force against you to overcome him. Meanwhile, all the other comics are telling mother-in-law jokes. Damn right he's a god to them.

* * *

In the last couple of years alone, three well-respected art houses in New York—MOMA (Museum of Modern Art), Maccarone Gallery, and Participant Inc.—have all launched retrospectives of Andy's work, along with major articles in both *The New York Times* and *The*

Huffington Post, thanks to the gargantuan efforts of fellow artist and curator Jonathan Berger. Today Kaufman is considered as important as Warhol. Add to this the release of his first comedy album in thirty-five years (thanks to Lynne), along with this book, and it's easy to see that Andy Kaufman gets more popular as the years go on than Frank Sinatra does. This new infusion of interest is directly tied to the film, and Danny DeVito, Ron Meyer, Stacey Snider, Jim Carrey, Milos Forman, Michael Hausman, George Shapiro, Howard West, Stacey Sher, Michael Shamberg, Lynne Margulies, Scott Alexander, and Larry Karaszewski should be applauded for keeping Andy alive today.

We need more renegades like Andy in all walks of life, willing to put principles before their wallets. Andy threw the gauntlet down, drew the line in the sand for every artist who has come since. Ask major comedians out there today and they'll all tell you how important Kaufman was and is in their development.

Let me give you an example of one of them: comedian Dave Chappelle. In 2005, Comedy Central announced that Dave Chappelle had quit, leaving behind his top-rated show on Comedy Central along with a $50 million contract. The industry was shocked. Who in his right mind would walk away from that kind of cash? And yet he did. Just got up and left. Obviously he had to be mad as a hatter or he made an ethical decision, but making an ethical decision over money in Hollywood means you *are* mad as a hatter. Why did he do it? Nobody knew.

Cut to the Aspen Comedy Festival, where the who's who of comedy royalty would meet every year for four days. One of the top events in 2005 was a fundraiser for the American Film Institute hosted at film producer Jon Peters's Aspen estate. About 150 guests attended and rumor had it that Dave Chappelle would make a rare appearance. I, like all guests, was transported to the party on a horse-drawn sleigh that briskly traveled up and down the snow-laden countryside while we were snugly wrapped in alpaca fur. The bells clustered around the neck of the Clydesdale announced a new visitor had arrived at the door, where we were greeted with a hot mug of cider. The interior of Peters's mansion was decked out for the Christmas season with a Christmas tree in every room. It was quite impressive to say the least.

Chappelle was on everyone's mind but was nowhere in sight. I was beginning to think that he was a no-show when I felt a tap on my shoulder. It was a tall, lean, no-messin'-around black man. He whispered in my ear, "Mr. Zmuda—Dave Chappelle would like to see you." I was led through the mansion to a section that had been shut off to the rest of the guests. I followed this stranger up through a series of stairways and turns culminating at a closed bedroom door. I could hear the sound of voices inside. The stranger knocked on the door with a special code and then opened it and gestured for me to step inside. There were only about four or five people in the room, most sitting on the edge of the bed smoking the wacky. One of them was Dave Chappelle. "ZMUDA! OK, everybody, here's the man I've been telling you about!" He got up and gave me the "soul brother" handshake. Another member of his entourage passed me the joint. I took a quick hit.

"Folks, listen up," Chappelle continued. "It was because of this man and Andy Kaufman that I quit my job!" For the life of me I didn't know where Chappelle was going with this. $50 million down the drain because of me. I wasn't sure this was such a good thing. I winced. "I did?"

"Damn straight, my brother," Chappelle said. "It was your book [referring to *Andy Kaufman Revealed!*]. I love that book. Everybody should read it," he said, then proudly announced to the others, "Him and Kaufman told the entire entertainment industry to fuck themselves! I did just what you and Andy did!" Everyone around agreed with Dave and looked at me as if I was some sort of white Eldridge Cleaver, high-fiving me and giving me more ganja. Dave continued, "Really, man, that book inspired me. Truly did. That show [he was referring to *Chappelle's Show* on Comedy Central] just wanted me to keep that same old step-and-fetch-it bullshit going.

I wasn't going to do it! I don't care how much they paid me. I got to do my own thing, like Andy did!" I joked and said, "Now Dave, let's not be too hasty! Fifty million dollars." Everyone laughed. I continued, "So how you doin'?" "Great, man. Really, Bob, that show was killin' me. Now I know how Andy was feeling having to do *Taxi*." There was a knock on the door. A voice said, "They're waiting for you, Dave." "Oh, yeah. I'm coming."

We all followed Chappelle as he left and proceeded back through the maze of halls until we got through to the main party. When the guests spotted him, the place went up with spontaneous applause. He worked his way up to a makeshift stage in front of a massive fireplace where a small band of musicians was waiting for him. He was handed a microphone and immediately went to work. He was on fire and kept everyone in stitches for the next twenty minutes and then ended his set rapping with the band.

Weeks later, I pieced together the rest of the story. It was true. *Chappelle's Show* was the hottest ticket on television. It was Comedy Central's jewel. But the audience, both in the studio and at home, was all white. They just loved Chappelle playing the "dumb street nigger" with cocaine all over his lips while he scratched himself anxiously for another fix. Funny as all hell, but to Dave's newfound Muslim friends back in Africa (Dave would travel there a lot), it was like, "What the hell you doin', man?"

It took a lot of courage for him to turn all that bread down and listen to his true self. Almost overnight because of what he did, he became a hero to the black community and his street cred rose considerably. Even the whites who miss the old shtick from the show cut him slack and admire him greatly. Nowadays he works whenever he likes, to sold-out audiences. Recently the new head of Comedy Central said, "We'd take him back whenever he wants and next time on his terms."

Dave sent a strong message to the rest of the comedy community: it's not about money. It's about what it is you want to say. Still, I must admit I miss that step-and-fetch-it stuff. Dave still incorporates it into his act but nowadays it doesn't become *the* act. Just when I thought the values of what Kaufman stood for were dead, a champion like Dave Chappelle steps forward and reminds me that there is still a real vanguard out there that can't be bought, just like Andy.

Dave Chappelle—$50 million. That's one heavy motherfucker! Of course, he does point out in his act that his wife is "just beginning to talk to him again."

Lynne

Very interesting! Because when that happened, when Chappelle walked away from his show, I thought, "Wow, that's so much like what Andy would have done!" Same with Joaquin Phoenix's movie I'm Still Here. *If that wasn't inspired by Kaufman, I'll eat pickled pig's feet. Not to mention Sacha Baron Cohen's* Borat. *And* Anchorman—*it seems that Will Ferrell has lifted a page straight out of Andy's "alter-ego" playbook and now promotes that successful franchise while not breaking character, à la Clifton. Don't get me started.*

*   *   *

"Dick Ebersol killed my son." These shocking and bitter words were a constant refrain from Stanley Kaufman. He was referring to the spat that Andy had with Dick Ebersol, producer of *Saturday Night Live,* which would lead to his being fired from the show and which subsequently, according to Stanley, is what got Andy terribly depressed, sick, and led to his death. The Kaufman/Ebersol Battle may be a case of, "I've made you. I can also break you."

First let's go back to 1975, when two young and untried producers, Lorne Michaels and Dick Ebersol, are casting a new late-night show for NBC called *Saturday Night Live.* At the time, late Saturday night was the worst time slot on television. The only reason the show came about is that some bean-counter in the advertising department at NBC figured out that more revenue could be gotten if they ran a live show as opposed to a pre-recorded program. Other than that, the network couldn't care less about SNL. Creatively there were no expectations whatsoever. Ebersol caught Andy's act at Budd Friedman's Improv. He was immediately hooked and brought Andy to the attention of his partner, Lorne, and SNL talent exec John Head. Lorne agreed and Kaufman was hired to be a semi-regular performer on SNL. Overnight, it would make him famous. Lorne, who was quite sophisticated, realized early on that Andy was so unusual in what he did that it was almost impossible to give him notes on whatever it was he was doing. After all, giving Andy notes would be akin to telling Picasso that perhaps his choice of colors wasn't correct. At best, Lorne could say, "Andy, make it longer" or "make it shorter." Other than that, Andy was totally left alone, safe in his own bizarre world.

Lorne stated:

I knew an essentially shy kid who had gone from his parents' home to a stage to national television. People would describe Andy as "quirky" or "idiosyncratic," all of which were euphemisms for "We weren't there yet." Nobody knew where he was headed, but it seemed really interesting. I think that the network at the time and the consciousness of what people would find acceptable was pretty sad. Andy was on the outside of what people were prepared to risk. But in late-night television, people did not mind it, and he was instantly popular. What I tried to do with him was to bring him along gently, so that he was always protected on the show. The cast was instantly supportive of him, a little less later on because during the second or third year, Andy would be doing pieces that could last a weekend and that meant that they wouldn't get to perform. But he was the first to begin to define anti-performance. He didn't really care whether the audience joined in or not. He was talking to himself out loud, basically, and if you wanted to tune in to the dialogue, it was perfectly all right with him. But he wasn't pleading with you to join in. It was conceptual and pure and, more importantly to me, it was what he wanted to do. I wish I could say it was popular. It was certainly popular in the small segment of society that I lived in. Back then, the kids in the '70s used to call it "Brechtian." It was anti-performance and therefore, sometimes the audience response was outrage or anger, which seemed to please him. I looked at it as if I was presenting a performance piece from Andy Kaufman. As for the wrestling, what happened was, as he became more and more committed to it, like people who develop an orthodoxy, it's very hard to get out of it, because you're pretty much heading down that road. And Andy passed the sort of safety exits three or four exits ago.

Jump ahead a few years and Lorne leaves the show and Dick Ebersol's now producing it. Andy shows up one day, Ebersol watches his bit and says no, he doesn't like it, and bumps Andy from that week's telecast. Apparently the two get into a loud shouting match. I wasn't there at the time, as I was off writing a Joel Schumacher film called *D.C. Cab* for Universal. Andy did call me a couple of weeks later and told me that he and Ebersol had mended fences and in fact Dick had come up with a funny idea for him. I said, "What's that?" Andy asked me if I had seen SNL a few months before, when they did a phone-in vote with viewers at home. It was to kill a lobster or to let it live. The lobster's name was Larry. With a boiling pot of water and a live lobster, votes were taken during the live telecast. Luckily for Louie, at the end of the show viewers voted to save his life. I told Andy I did see the segment. What did this have to do with him? "Well, what Dick wants to do," he said, "is to have another vote. This time, they vote if I live or die." "Live or die?" I asked. Andy answered, "Vote to keep me on the show or off. Same thing, I guess." I immediately said, "They're going to vote you off." Andy said, "You think so?" I said, "I know so. Comedically, if they voted to save the lobster, the next bastard they vote on is going down. It's only logical." He laughed. "That will be great." I said, "I'm missing something here. How is getting voted off of SNL a good thing?" "Because," he said, "Dick and I agreed that if I do get voted off ..." Once again I repeated, "Not *if*—you will." He said, "Fine. Once they vote me off, a few weeks later, Dick's going to call me and I'll appear back on the show either first as a guy sweeping up in the background or as Tony Clifton." I said, "That's funny."

So on November 20, 1982, they vote and—as expected— Kaufman is voted off. Everything is going as planned, but then a strange thing happens—Ebersol never calls Kaufman as promised. And any time Andy calls him, he refuses to take the call; i.e., Ebersol double-crosses Andy. He really is cut from the show— FOREVER! Everyone in the Kaufman camp, including myself, is shocked and appalled by Ebersol's behavior. Marty Klein, Andy's agent at APA, tries to reason with Dick, but to no avail. George Shapiro, Andy's manager, doesn't fare much better. Andy was furious. He even wanted to sue Ebersol and NBC. He felt he had to do something. Immediately ticket sales for our college dates began to drop drastically, as SNL was such a powerful cultural program that people were going to believe what they heard. Andy was DOA.

*   *   *

What I've found astonishing all these years, and nobody other than myself has really picked up on it, is the willingness on the part of Lorne Michaels and the cast of *Taxi* to play themselves in the film. Weren't they aware that Scott and Larry's script portrays them as antagonists to Kaufman, our anti-hero? They are, after all, the Inquisition to Kaufman the artist. Didn't they know they were being cast as the heavies?

If the script didn't convey that to them when they read it, or perhaps they only read their parts, then surely a brief analysis of Milos's films should have given them a clue. Think about it. Milos only does films where the hero, be he Amadeus, Jack Nicholson in

One Flew Over the Cuckoo's Nest, Larry Flynt, or Andy Kaufman are castigated by the society they live in. In *Man on the Moon,* these antagonists are the cast of *Taxi,* SNL, and the maniacal network executive played brilliantly by the late Vincent Schiavelli. But who in their right mind would portray themselves in such a light? The actors I could understand—a big Universal film directed by Milos Forman. How do you turn that down? But Lorne Michaels? Lorne didn't strike me as the type of person whose ego made him want to see himself on the big screen. With his portfolio he could probably buy Universal. Why then? To what end? Besides, it was Dick Ebersol who actually appeared on SNL and read the statement against Andy, not Lorne. It is bad enough that Dick goes down in history as the guy who dumped Kaufman. Why should Lorne get caught up in the controversy? He wasn't even attached to the show when the "vote" happened. Besides, if anyone supported Andy's work it was Michaels. I recently asked Scott Alexander why Lorne played the Dick Ebersol role. He told me because Lorne was in an earlier scene, so they just decided not to throw too many SNL producers at the film-going audience as it might confuse them. Besides, Bob, "It's only a fucking movie." I had to laugh. He was right. But still, if you lived through the reality of "the vote" like Lynne, George, Stanley Kaufman, and I did and saw how deeply it injured Andy, you had to take it seriously. It was the second time in his life that Andy felt dumped, the first being when he thought his grandfather had dumped him. As Stanley would say about the vote, "Andy never fully recovered from it."

Now, to be fair, I could see why Ebersol got upset with Andy. Kaufman found SNL downright boring. I would watch him watch the TV monitor in his dressing room and just stare at the sketches going out live. He never smiled once. They just didn't register. And yet America was going crazy for the stuff. The show and cast had really taken off. Andy would get on a chair and reach up to the monitor mounted high on the wall and change the channel—looking for cartoons or, better yet, wrestling. Now that's something he could relate to. Did Ebersol perhaps walk into Andy's dressing room once too often and see his precious programming turned off while Andy looked for Popeye cartoons?

Or even worse. How about when Ebersol couldn't even get into Andy's dressing room to talk to him because of that "fucking meditation." Andy would meditate for twenty minutes before every performance. Never missed it. Ever. It didn't matter if it was SNL. There always was a huge sign on his door: "Meditating—Do Not Disturb."

Lynne

He did it at Taxi *too. First of all, he had it in his contract that he didn't have to be there for the week of rehearsals that the rest of the cast had to do. Andy had a stand-in for the week, and only had to show up on Friday for the dress rehearsal before the show. (He could memorize the script after one reading.) So that alone drove the rest of the cast crazy. And then, while they were all out on the stage for dress rehearsal, they'd be waiting for Andy while he was in his dressing room meditating. I remember being in there meditating with Andy and Tony Danza pounding on the door yelling, "Andy, get the fuck out here!" I glanced up at Andy and he had the tiniest little smile on his face while he continued meditating. He loved driving people mad.*

When he walked out on that stage in front of all those "LIVE" cameras being beamed out to millions of viewers, what they were seeing was basically a man still in a "trance," or at the very least just coming out of one. He wasn't even operating on this physical plane! The mere fact that he was able to get away with this for as long as he did is in itself a miracle. I could only imagine what might have been going on in Dick Ebersol's mind when he finally figured it out:

E: You're not eating up my precious time reaching nirvana on my show, not when Clearasil commercials are going for twenty-five thousand dollars for thirty seconds. Pack up your 'mantra' and get the hell out of here! We take comedy seriously here at SNL.

A: If you take it so seriously, why isn't it funny?"

E: Not funny to you, perhaps, because you're a weirdo.

A: I laugh at Laurel and Hardy, Abbott and Costello, and W.C. Fields! I laughed when Eddie Murphy would say, "I'm Gumby, damn it."

E: Any other time on SNL?

A: Probably not.

E: Andy, do you know how insulting it is for you to find the other cast members who work hard all week not funny?

A: I'm sorry. Do you want me to lie and make believe I'm laughing? Can I keep my job then?

E: It's too late, Andy. You've got to go. You're just not a team player.

A: The cast of *Taxi* could have told you that. I've never fit in anywhere. It's not my nature. That doesn't make me a bad person. It's just how I am. Sorry.

E: Well, we're sorry too. Just pack up your congas and wrestling mat and leave.

A: But where am I supposed to go? I've been doing this show since the beginning.

E: Go over to David Letterman. He'll put you on.

A: There you have it. David Letterman finds me funny. Explain that one.

E: I don't have to explain anything. I just want you out of here. NOW GO! Or I'll have you thrown out. I don't have time for this. I have a show to produce.

A: Maybe that's why your show isn't funny! It's just become big business. It's not fun anymore.

E: SECURITY!

A: Can I say one last thing?

E: NO!

A: Just one and then I'll leave.

E: What is it?

A: If I've made one person happy, it's all been worth it.

E: GET THE FUCK OUT OF HERE!

Dick Ebersol knew that SNL sensibility was nothing more than *Second City* sketch comedy (*Second City* being a comedy troupe out of Chicago that 80 percent of SNL's cast came out of). Kaufman, on the other hand, was too esoteric, some say dadaistic. He made an audience think. Christ, TV was supposed to be a sedative—at least Marshall McLuhan told us so in his book *The Medium Is the Message*. Andy was stirring things up too much. Beside, Ebersol's Frankenstein monster was beginning to talk back to his creator, and nobody talked back to Ebersol. Kaufman had to go, and what better way than to have the audience vote him off. It was the perfect cover, and Ebersol could walk away clean, or so he thought.

> Hi. I'm Dick Ebersol, the executive producer of *Saturday Night Live*. In recent weeks we have received inquiries from many of you, including even the editors of *TV Guide*, as to why, prior to our last two telecasts, we heavily promoted Andy Kaufman and then failed to present him as advertised. So tonight, let me set the record straight by saying, in my opinion, that in both cases Andy misled us into thinking, right up until airtime, that his material would be up to the show's standards. It was not. It was not even funny, and in my opinion Andy Kaufman is not funny anymore. *[Audience applause.]* And I believe you, the audience here, agrees with me. *[More applause.]* So thank you, and I hope this sets the record straight. Good night.

I have a problem with Dick's rejecting Kaufman's material as "not funny." By then, there were certainly enough articles in major publications like the *New York Times, Rolling Stone, Village Voice,* etc., that labeled Andy the anti-comedian, and his material was known at times to cause more controversy than yuks. What I think really happened back then was that SNL was under vicious attacks in the press for not being funny itself. The pressure on Ebersol to deliver the funny every week had to be enormous.

Andy worked best in juxtaposition to the "funny." In comedy clubs where he started, you had a series of comedians, one after another. When Andy got up and did what he did, it was so different. You found yourself laughing because it was so out of place. When SNL was funny during the Lorne Michaels years, you could drop Andy in the middle of it all and once again, the juxtaposition made it work. When SNL started going downhill comedically—plop Andy in the middle of that and the anti-comedy stuff doesn't fly as well, because everything around him is anti-comedy; i.e., not funny.

There's another scenario that I recently discovered that could just be the smoking gun and may have played a big part in the

Kaufman/Ebersol debacle. And that is the "other" late-night comedy sketch show, *Fridays. Fridays* was ABC's rip-off of SNL. It aired
Friday nights live on ABC and was an exact duplicate of SNL in
every way. At first, Ebersol shrugged it off as a joke, but over time,
SNL ratings went down and *Fridays* ratings started to rise, especially when a certain performer would make an appearance. That
performer was none other than Andy Kaufman. His appearances
on *Fridays* became so controversial that all of America would be
talking about it the next day around the office water cooler. In fact,
according to John Moffitt, the executive producer of *Fridays,* Andy
actually saved the show from being canceled:

> It was the end of our first season and ABC informed us they were
> not picking us up. Since we had nothing to lose, we went for broke
> and asked Andy to appear on the live show, telling him he could
> do anything he wanted to. That's when he refused to read the
> cue cards and got into a fight with the cast and crew. It was real
> fisticuffs and we had to cut to commercial. The next day, that's
> all Americans were talking about—Was it real? Was it staged? I
> immediately got a call from ABC telling us how fantastic it was
> for ratings and that they'd changed their minds and decided to
> pick us up for another year … So we have Andy to thank.

I believe that after hearing this, Ebersol went through the roof.
Here he is, the guy who discovered Kaufman, and Kaufman goes
over to the enemy. Ebersol had to be furious with him, and I believe
this may have played a big part in his wanting Andy dumped from
SNL.

So I can understand where Dick was coming from. What I take
issue with is his not returning Kaufman's calls. That's the double-
cross. That was mean.

My theory of *Fridays* being the culprit that pissed Ebersol off to
start with may be substantiated in this interview Lynne had with
Howard West, the rarely seen or heard other half of Shapiro/West.

Howard: I was against his doing the vote.

Lynne: What was his thinking behind doing it?

Howard: That he'd be back in the good graces of Lorne Michaels and he'd be back in the good graces of the public again ... WRONG. Also "something" came down between George and Dick Ebersol.

I believe *Fridays* was that "something" and why Andy felt he had to get back in the good graces of Lorne Michaels. What did he do to Lorne Michaels? Was Lorne also pissed that Andy went over to the other side (*Fridays*)?

If what I suspect to be true is true and *Fridays* is the smoking gun, you'll never hear Shapiro/West admit it. If so, then *they*, not Andy, created the powder-keg situation that led to Andy's being let go. Maybe instead of spooning chocolate ice cream down his piehole during business meetings, Kaufman should have been listening more.

*   *   *

Andy didn't like being a "star." It separated him from normal, everyday people and he detested the feeling of him "being better than anyone else." That's why at the height of his career, he took a lowly busboy job at Jerry's Deli for minimum wage while pulling in $40,000 a week on *Taxi*. As Martin Scorsese said, "It's nice to be the center of attention; the danger is it may alter your perceptions. The most important thing for an actor is their sense of the relationships between people. This social behavior I find fascinating, and very often if you walk into a room and you're the center of attention, it's harder to pick up on these things." No wonder the cast of *Taxi* was pissed at Kaufman. Every Monday night is when they would go off to a fancy restaurant and party, which usually meant drinking and doing drugs, which Andy wouldn't partake in.

He would tell them he couldn't join them because he had to work at his busboy job Monday nights. They must have thought, "Well, fuck him—isn't his *Taxi* family more important than cleaning up some stranger's slop?"

Back then Andy saw it coming. He saw it when Danny got rid of his old car and they all started signing autographs. Saw it when they stopped renting in Hollywood Hills and bought property in Bel Air and Malibu. Saw it when they couldn't be seen at Canter's (a low-rent Jewish deli) anymore. Saw it when they were becoming rich and now were swept into keeping up with the Joneses. Except now the Joneses had fourteen-bedroom homes with a personal workout gym and pool. Andy wondered how the hell he'd gotten caught up in this mindless pursuit of the almighty buck. It's one of the reasons why when he supposedly died, his family found all these uncashed checks from his wrestling bouts in Memphis. He loved it so much he didn't want to take money for it. It made him think back to how his dad would berate him, telling him he had to make something out of his life. Now that he had, he could just as easily have drunk the Kool-Aid like everyone else. If that was the case, he might as well have just joined the jewelry business with his dad, just like his dad did with his dad before him. He wanted out and what faster way to get out than death itself?

In an interview that Andy did with talk-show host Tom Cottle, Cottle asked him point-blank if his rejection of Hollywood, or the whole body politic of the U.S. for that matter, was going to cost him in the end.

> Cottle: Let me ask you, Andy, and I don't want to keep harping on this that you're weird or anything, but the—are you—are you gonna pay some price or have you felt that you're paying a price, NOT being the typical company guy, the organization guy, doing what everybody else does, getting into the lifestyle that everybody else does?

Kaufman: If I was like that, I don't think I could do what I do! If I was just regular normal, I wouldn't be able to do the things that I do when I'm performing. Like my Elvis Presley imitation is the result of being alone for a year. I think it was 1966 or '67 when Elvis was at a low point. You know, he did go through several years of being considered a has-been by most of the country except for the South, 'cause I remember I was in New York growing up and I was the only one that I knew that liked Elvis Presley at the time. That's when the Beatles were popular and a whole new kind of music took over until 1969 when he [Elvis] made his comeback so I was the only one that liked him and I would stay home most of the time and just play his records and imitate him, adopted him as a character, combed my hair like him, dressed like him in school. All my friends would call me Elvis, y'know, but it was—it was not at a time when he was popular at all! And people would laugh at me and scoff at me if I said I liked Elvis Presley! So because I had this taste that was different from other people, I was able to work on this unknowingly, not knowing that I would later become a performer, I was actually working on my Elvis Presley imitation most of the day for one year.

Cottle: How did you feel when Elvis Presley died?

Kaufman: I was sad and, uh, you know, like everybody else, y'know. I was a little—doubting whether it was true or not ..."

Obviously one can see where the spark that ignited his faking his death idea came from. He was fascinated with the idea that Elvis faked his death. Not for a moment did he believe Elvis did, but he knew a good idea when he heard one. Besides, Elvis's career was at an all-time low when he died, just like Andy's. It was as if Elvis's and Andy's career trajectory was at the same place: zero. If Elvis couldn't fake his death, Andy would. He had to. If he'd stuck around, he'd be swept into the mindless vortex of Hollywood like everybody else. And being like everyone else was the worst thing that could ever happen to him. Being different was his pride and joy. It's what made him a star, but at the same time it was a double-edged sword. America liked him strange but not *too* strange. The crazy uncle would be invited to the Christmas party but when he started to shit himself, he was unceremoniously asked to leave. Andy not only shit himself, he started making sculptures out of his doo-doo. Uncle Andy had to leave the building.

*   *   *

The camera lights were blinding me as I was painting a web of fascination about Kaufman for a cute MTV interviewer. That, along with the fact that my vanity made me remove my glasses, meant I didn't see the figure enter the room. He sat in the back and absorbed my Kaufman tales with fascination. When the camera lights went off and the interview ended, I reached inside my jacket for my specs, put them on, and saw him sitting there. It was comedian Robert Klein. He was to be interviewed after me for something on MTV I've since forgotten. When I drew near him, he said, "ZMU-DA. ZMU-DA. The man whose name is missing a vowel. It should be ZA-MUDA." I said, "Hi, Robert." He had appeared on my Comic Relief charity program in the past, so I knew him somewhat. "Great stories," he said. "Thanks," I said. Then it seemed like he needed to get something off his chest. He blurted out, "You know, nobody would give a damn about Kaufman if it wasn't for you." I said, "I beg your pardon?" "It's true," he continued. "Andy was a minor talent, but thanks to you, he's achieved legendary status." At first, I wasn't sure how to take it. Surely it was a backhanded compliment.

Klein said, "Don't get me wrong. Andy was a lovely guy. I liked him. We often talked. But you're taking him to a whole new level." I said, "He died young and should be recognized for his work." He countered, "Well, Za-muda, you're a good friend. I hope his family appreciates all you're doing for his memory." "Oh yeah," I said. "They do."

I lied. The Kaufmans, or, as they like to call themselves nowadays, the "Andy Kaufman Memorial Trust," view Lynne and me as the enemy. They haven't a clue as to the years of hard work she and I have put in to keep Andy out there in the public eye. They erroneously believe that America just woke up one sunny morning and decided their brother was a comedy icon. Yeah, sure. And Lana Turner was discovered at Schwab's!

When I asked one of the Universal executives, "Why did you take a risk on the Kaufman movie?" he laughed and said, "What risk? You already got an Emmy nomination on the NBC special and the ratings were good. That gave us a nice warm feeling as to where we could spend our money." Not to mention that Lynne's doc *I'm from Hollywood* for quite a few years enjoyed the title of "Most Watched Show" in the history of the Comedy Channel, as well as being named in *Time* magazine's "Top 10 on TV" in 1992.

It took me years to "condition" the public to Andy's brilliance and now, with the movie coming out, I put the pedal to the metal. When I wrote *Andy Kaufman Revealed!*, my publicist at the time, Jodee Blanco, set up a cross-country tour paid for by Universal and Little, Brown books where I would speak on campuses during the day and do book signings at night. Lynne and I co-directed an A&E *Biography* and did a retrospective on Kaufman. When it came out, *Variety* said, "The Andy Kaufman *Biography* was the best of the whole series." By now, people were being "conditioned" to think about Kaufman again, and *E! True Hollywood Story*, not wanting to be left out, called and asked for footage. Why not? I was determined to make Andy the star he always wanted to be. I didn't let the fact that he was supposedly dead stand in my way. I would

keep Andy alive until his return. I am a company man and have
worked diligently for my boss going on forty years now. Did I get
a gold watch or even a thank you from the Kaufman estate? Hell,
no. Instead, the opposite took place. The family—or I should say
the "Andy Kaufman Memorial Trust"—turned on me. First, they
hated the movie, then Clifton, and then they hated my book. In
fact, Andy's sister, Carol, called me in a rage, yelling at me, "How
could you talk about Andy's sex life? It was disgusting." I told her,
"Don't be so prudish. Andy had a great sex life and it should be
applauded." At first I thought the Kaufmans were having a hard
time adjusting to the fact that Andy now belonged to the public.
But I soon realized something else was going on and maybe it
didn't have to do with Andy or me or any of us. Maybe it had to
do with the Kaufmans themselves.

When the Kaufmans heard of Andy's condition, they all flew
out to be with him—Stanley, mother Janice, Michael, and Carol.
The first thing Andy decided to do was put them all, including
himself, in family counseling. Sound strange? Not if you knew
Andy. Since they arrived on his doorstep, and this might be the
last roundup, he had a few things he wanted to say. So he hired
fellow TM-er John Gray, the same therapist who later wrote the
bestseller *Men Are From Mars, Women Are From Venus,* who was
holding family death counselings at the time. He was pretty much
a New Age therapist. This was for people who knew they were
dying and wanted to get it all off their chests before they went
(something Andy would do even knowing he was faking his death).
Remember, he said he'd return in twenty to thirty years, which
meant he wouldn't be talking to them for a long, long time. He had
a lot to unload. Lynne told me the sessions, which she occasionally attended, became screaming sessions on Andy's part, letting
them know he wasn't very pleased with them. Andy also brought
in his manager, George Shapiro, and gave him a tongue-lashing
too, basically letting him know that he felt George wasn't supportive of his creativity, and that because of them he would soon

die never achieving the stature that he felt he deserved. Stanley said, "Dr. Gray was important to Andy. We went through two to three boxes of Kleenex per session."

When I heard about the sessions, I asked Andy if he wanted me there. He said, "Absolutely not. You and Lynne were the only ones who supported me wholeheartedly." It was that kind of mutual support I also received from Andy ever since I'd known him. If he was going to die, which he supposedly did on May 16, 1984, I took it upon myself to keep the home fires burning until his return.

I started by bringing Tony Clifton back on the one-year anniversary of his supposed death. Clifton would make an appearance at Mitzi Shore's The Comedy Store. (They used it as the ending for the film.) So I hired a full-time publicist, and then I hit the airwaves, doing any cockamamie radio station that would have me. I worked it tirelessly for six months, made the anniversary a fundraiser for the American Cancer Society (since Andy supposedly died of cancer), and even corralled a bunch of comedy celebrities to attend, such as Lily Tomlin, Whoopi Goldberg, Robin Williams, Eddie Murphy, etc. When Clifton hit the stage, everyone went crazy, thinking, "Could it be true?" Remember, back then nobody even suspected that I had been playing Clifton all those years, as it hadn't come out yet. To add to the mystery, I stood in the audience myself applauding Clifton with everyone else. People left The Comedy Store that night stunned. Had Kaufman returned?

Another incredible thing happened that night also. The charity Comic Relief was born. Like I said, it was the first charity event I ever mounted, and it just so happened that around the same time across the pond, a man by the name of Bob Geldof had mounted a gigantic charitable music concert called Live Aid. It was on everybody's radar. My ex-comedy team partner Chris Albrecht had just landed a job at HBO, his title being senior vice president, original programming, West Coast. I went to see him, and soon we mounted the Live Aid version of comedy, Comic Relief, hosted by Robin Williams, Whoopi Goldberg, and Billy Crystal. With my new title of president and founder of Comic Relief, and now HBO utilizing me in their in-house publicity department, I was able to do more press, this time on somebody else's nickel. Although my main job was to speak about the charity and Williams's, Crystal's, and Goldberg's contributions, sooner or later the interviewer couldn't wait to hear Kaufman stories. I kept Andy out there in every interview I did from 1984 to the present. Hundreds of interviews. I even worked him into every Comic Relief we did on HBO.

Slowly but surely, because of all of this, Andy's career began to rise from the ashes. It took a momentous leap years after Kaufman's supposed death, when Shapiro and West were producing the hottest show on TV, *Seinfeld.* I had read in the trades that NBC was renegotiating Seinfeld's contract, which I realized would have put Howard and George in a good position to get other products on the air. I persuaded them to go with me to Rick Ludwin, head of specials at NBC, to pitch a comedy salute to Andy Kaufman. Rick had to take the meeting. No way was he going to insult Howard and George. But doing a prime-time, one-hour comedy salute to a sit-com performer who had supposedly died ten years earlier? A ludicrous proposal to Ludwin. But I had two cards up my sleeve. One was that in 1992, on the eighth anniversary of Andy's supposed passing, which was Comic Relief V, I had seized that opportunity to capture every major comedian on the show to tell his or her favorite Kaufman story to my behind-the-scenes documentary crew. My friend and executive producer, John Davies, and I then edited up a great ten-minute "sizzle reel" for Ludwin to see all these big stars talking about Andy. Robin, Whoopi, Billy, Letterman, Jay Leno, Chris Rock … the list was endless. Since this was going to be basically a "clip" show anyway, half of everything we needed was already in the can. Ludwin was pretty impressed, but still leery. When he stated, "It's been ten years. I don't know if kids today would remember him," that was the cue I had been waiting for and pulled the second ace out of my sleeve. I played him the number-one song on the charts. It was R.E.M.'s *Man on the Moon.*

I handed him a lyrics sheet. Rick was amazed. "I love this song. I didn't know it was about Andy."

> *Mott the Hoople and the game of Life*
> *Yeah, yeah, yeah, yeah*
> *Andy Kaufman in a wrestling match*
> *Yeah, yeah, yeah, yeah*

That year we shot *A Comedy Salute to Andy Kaufman* for NBC. Not only was it a critical success, but it was even nominated for an Emmy. The one-hour special aired in prime time to great ratings. I even flew in Michael Kaufman, Andy's brother, and Andy's daughter, Maria, to end the show. Kaufman was back, thanks to yours truly.

Others, of course, helped me to mount the comedy salute, including Davies, a brilliant producer in his own right, along with author Bill Zehme, RJ Johnson, Phil Kruener, and Bibbi Herrman. And Shapiro/West's power position didn't hurt, either. But at the end of the day, my Comic Relief footage, with the biggest stars in comedy, did the trick. You see, I never stopped working for my boss. And when he returns, he's going to owe me thirty years of back pay. Hear that, Andy?

CHAPTER 7

Faking Death

Ring ...

B: Hello?

A: Bob, it's Andy.

B: Andy, it's four a.m.

A: Sorry, but I decided to do it.

B: *[Groggy]* Do what?

A: Fake my death.

B: Great! Call me tomorrow.

A: Bob, I'm not joking. I shouldn't even be saying this over the phone. Can you meet me at Canter's?

B: You mean now?

A: Yeah, it's important. This might be the most important day in my entire career.

[Thirty minutes later, I'm nursing a bowl of matzo-ball soup. Kaufman arrives ten minutes later. He sits down and orders a bowl of chocolate ice cream.]

B: That stuff's gonna kill you.

A: I'm a dead man anyway. *[He laughs.]* OK, here's what we need to do.

B: Stop right there, white man. What do you mean "we"? Andy, if I told you once I told you a thousand times: I think your faking your death is brilliant, and I know if anyone can pull it off, it's you. But if you're truly serious about doing it, you've got to count me out. This is one put-on I can't help you with.

A: Why not?

B: Well, for one thing, it's illegal. People fake their deaths every day.

A: They do?

B: Of course they do. Some of them don't want to pay alimony or child support, or they're looking to rip off the insurance company on their death benefits. Andy, you're in SAG, AFTRA, the Writers Guild. Your dad probably has a large death benefit on you already. If you come up dead, those companies are going to pay large death payoffs to your family, especially since you're so young. If they find out you're not really dead, you'll probably get a jail sentence.

A: But they're not going to find out.

B: But if they do, you'll be in a hell of a lot of trouble. And I'm not going to be in it with you. Besides, if you really go ahead with this, you shouldn't tell anyone, especially me. It's that special. Besides, you can't ask me to lie to your mother about you being dead when you're not. It would kill her. I couldn't do that.

[I could see what I was telling him was beginning to get through to him.]

B: Andy, if you do this, really do it, you've got to convince even me that you really died. If you can do that, you've achieved the greatest put-on of all time.

A: Convince you?

B: Yes, convince me. And seeing that we've been talking about this for three years now, I don't know how that is remotely possible.

A: Well, I see I have my work cut out for me then.

Two years later, Andy Kaufman died. I went to his funeral. I didn't shed a tear. In fact, I had to bite my lip a few times to keep from exploding in laughter. At one point, I looked over to Bob Morton (Morty) a few pews over. Morty was a good friend of Andy's and was the executive producer of the *Letterman* show. I think he was biting his lip too, trying not to laugh. Everyone was expecting Andy to jump out of the casket at any time. I knew he wouldn't—that would have been too easy. Besides, being in it for the long run (thirty years), Kaufman would never give the trick away. He was old-school wrestling. You never admitted hoaxes … ever. It was a sacred code between the wrestlers back then and Kaufman. Lynne and I adhered to the same code.

I know this must all sound strange to the layman. But those of you who know about "the code" understand exactly what I'm talking about and how one would go to the grave keeping the secrets. Many have. The only reason I'm giving it up now is that Andy set a time limit on this one. Thirty years. So I've kept my part of the bargain and kept my mouth shut. But no more. The prank's over. I want him back and he's coming back.

Lynne, on the other hand—I really can't tell if she is in on it or not. Her thinking I'm insane believing Andy's alive might just be her working reverse psychology on me. She now believes the "secret" Andy made her and me promise to keep from his parents may just be the tip of the iceberg. His being gay was just half the story.

I'd be lying if I said the other half didn't cross my mind also. It had crossed many others' minds as well. But the mere thought of it was so forbidden, so unspeakable, no one dared utter the words. Lynne said, "Why was he so insistent that his parents never know?" Was the secret even darker than we all imagined?

I leafed through the book I had written about Andy nearly fourteen years ago and I listed it then, but more to scoff at the possibility than anything else. Was I wrong? Had the truth been staring me in the face for so long and my own personal homophobic denial made it more than I wanted to bear? Somewhere in my psyche was it a lot easier to believe he faked his death than to face such a horrible possibility? Did Andy Kaufman, in fact, die on May 16, 1984, and did he die of AIDS?

I didn't want to believe it. No, it was all too horrible to comprehend. Therefore, it must not be true. Yet it crossed everyone's mind who knew Andy, if even for a millisecond. But in the case of Lynne, those milliseconds added up to minutes and then hours, months, years, fueled by the knowledge of his being gay. Was this large-cell carcinoma, in fact, the AIDS virus misread at the time? After all, in '84 not much was known of the disease. People were dying from it, but nobody had put two and two together yet. It wasn't until a year after Kaufman's death that Rock Hudson was diagnosed with AIDS, and only then did people first begin to take it seriously. Hudson was considered the first celebrity to die of AIDS. Could Kaufman have been the first instead? What were the signs? Could he have contracted it during his sexual experimentation with males in the Castro, as Lynne had suggested, or did he pick it up at the Mustang Ranch from a hooker? Before AIDS, brothels really didn't enforce the "condom rule" as they legally do now. Would it somehow be easier on me if I knew Andy contracted it from a woman instead of a man? Would I think less of him if it was a male? Damn, why couldn't he have just faked his fucking death and that be the end of it? Why couldn't well enough be left alone? And yet, should Lynne and I hide from the truth no matter how horrible it could be? Why couldn't Kaufman's life be like that nice and tidy film Scott and Larry wrote? Why couldn't all our lives be like a Hollywood movie with a beautiful score by R.E.M. and a lovable Paul Giamatti playing me and a $20 million movie star like Jim Carrey playing Andy? Why couldn't everyone just leave well enough alone? Why couldn't Kaufman live on in people's minds as that funny Latka fellow from *Taxi* or that zany oddball who lip-synced to Mighty Mouse on SNL?

The answer was, Because Andy was real. A great artist whose work influenced countless other artists and will for years to come. And it's the job and responsibility of those who knew and loved him to bear witness to the truth and be honest about his life no matter how painful that truth may be. He belongs to history now, so let's lay it down right.

Toward the end, Lynne told me, the doctors gave him radiation that relieved the pressure of the tumors. Tumors caused by metastasis of lung cancer, which she believes may have been caused by AIDS. I, on the other hand, believe the tumors the doctors were looking at belonged to someone else's X-rays. He wasn't easy to be with at the end either. Nobody in that state is. He was pissed off he was dying this way. After all, he had so much more to do. He was just getting started. Only thirty-four years old. Was this some form of cosmic joke? At times, he'd break into mad laughter about it, and at other times, he'd openly weep. And yet somehow, Lynne stood by him. The woman should have been given a medal. The Kaufmans wouldn't have even been there when he supposedly died if Lynne hadn't called them. Andy didn't want his family to know he had cancer or even be with him at the end. She said, "He was REALLY pissed at me when I called them in for what would be his final days. He wanted to die in peace."

*   *   *

"On June 5, 1984 [twenty days after Andy Kaufman's reported death], a fifty-eight-year-old man went to his doctor's office to learn the results of a biopsy of a purple spot on his neck. He was told that it was Kaposi's sarcoma. The man's name was Rock Hudson. One year later, as his doctor, Michael Gottlieb, watched the actor's helicopter land atop UCLA Medical Center heliport, Gottlieb walked down to the hospital auditorium where countless reporters gathered. He stood up to a podium with a microphone. He knew he needed to be deliberate in every word he spoke. More than anything else, he did not want to sound embarrassed. That he knew was what had been the problem all along with this infernal epidemic. It was about sex, and it was about homosexuals. Taken all together, it had simply 'embarrassed' everyone, he knew, and tens of thousands of Americans would die because of it. It was time for people to stop being 'embarrassed,' Gottlieb decided, if our society was ever to beat this horrible enemy. In calm, firm tones, Gottlieb began reading from his prepared statement. 'Mr. Hudson is being evaluated and treated for complications of Acquired Immune Deficiency Syndrome—AIDS.'"

That haunting passage is from a remarkable book, *And the Band Played On*, by Randy Shilts, and I wonder if that same embarrassment lay at the core of Andy Kaufman's mysterious disappearance. All this talk of faking his death or not may be nothing more than misdirection from the real illusion that had taken place.

Why is it when Michelle Maccarone (owner of Maccarone Gallery in New York City, the art house that was mounting a retrospective of Andy's work and recognizing him as an important artist) went to see Andy's dad, Stanley, thinking he would be overjoyed with the news, instead heard him belligerently scoff, saying, "Why do a retrospective on him? He wasn't an artist. He was a troublemaker." His own dad. Did Stanley know what Lynne was implying? Did he know about Andy's being gay? Had he himself considered AIDS too? Was war hero Stanley Kaufman himself too embarrassed by what his son might have been into? Months later, after Michelle met with him, Stanley Kaufman himself would die, taking to his own grave secrets still unspoken, secrets that Lynne and I could now reveal.

*   *   *

Ring …

A: Hello … *cough … cough*

B: Andy, it's Bob. Stop with the coughing already. I think it's a dead giveaway.

A: I don't know. Everyone seems to believe it.

B: Can you talk?

A: Wait one second. I want to make sure Lynne can't hear … *[pause]* … It's OK. She's in the other room with the TV on. What's up?

B: Andy, you can't tell people you're dying because you ate too much chocolate.

A: Who told you that?

B: Little Wendy.

A. She did?

B: Yes … and so did Cathy Utman.

A: Well, I read this book called *Sugar Blues*. And it said too much chocolate can kill you. And Bob, you know nobody eats more chocolate than me. So I'm telling people that's what's killing me.

B: Well, quit telling them that. It sounds ludicrous. Nobody's going to believe you if you tell them that.

A: But the book said!!

B: Andy, I don't care about the book. Do you want people to believe you're dying?

A: Yes.

B: OK. Then don't go telling people that chocolate-covered Cocoa Puffs did you in.

A: What should I tell them?

B: Don't ask me. It's your death. You figure it out.

A: Maybe I'll just stick with the cancer.

B: Stick with the cancer. I like the cancer. So let me ask you, how long are you going to stay dead for?

A: Good question. I told Lynne if I was going to be a little boy about it, I'd go in hiding for one or two years. But if I was going to be a man about it, it'd be twenty to thirty years.

B: THIRTY YEARS!?! YOU CAN'T BE SERIOUS!

A: Well, think about it. Everyone knows I'm always pulling pranks. They'd expect me to disappear for a year or two, maybe even three or four. But if I'm gone for say twenty to thirty years, they'll really believe I died.

B: That's true. But your career will be over.

A: It's over now. Besides, did I tell you George was trying to get me on another sitcom? I'd rather be dead. If showbiz is no longer fun, I'd rather be doing something else anyway.

B: Andy, do you know how long thirty years is? It's a lifetime. What are you going to do over all that time?

A: I don't know, but it'll certainly be fun starting from scratch.

B: Christ, Andy, in thirty years people might not even remember who you are. So what's the point?

A: Well, that's the risk I'll have to take. If it looks like I'm being forgotten, I might come back earlier.

B: This is crazy.

A: I know. It's the best idea I've ever had. There's nothing else I can ever do to top it. How do I not go for it? Bob, I've thought about this for two to three years. Now there's no turning back. I'm gonna die.

B: Are you going to tell George about this?

A: NO!!! No commission for thirty years. I don't think he'd like that.

B: So Lynne doesn't know?

A: Nope, she thinks I'm really sick but I'm not taking it seriously.

B: Well, you better start acting like you're taking it seriously or she's not going to believe it if you don't.

A: She will. I have that figured out too. Believe me, it all works out in the long run.

CHAPTER 8

The Bombing Routine

I wrote a Joel Schumacher film years ago called *D.C. Cab* with a terrific writer named Gary Rosen. In it, we used the line, "What makes you can also break you." This line captures the predicament Andy was in. He was damned if he did and damned if he didn't. He had pushed the envelope as far as it could go. They were not going to let him explore any more. He was scaring people. Sure, he could have gotten on another sitcom easy enough. But he didn't want to. The writing was on the wall. He knew what he had to do. He had to pull off the greatest illusion of his career, faking his death, only this time everyone would be watching. I'd be watching. This time they'd want to frisk him and make sure there wasn't a trap door. They just didn't trust him anymore no matter what he said. And when he made his move, they went, "We know how you did that." Andy—you didn't die—you faked it—we caught you. Like Cindy Williams said when she heard he was dead: She laughed and told her husband, "Don't believe a word of it. He's not dead. He's pulling off one of his pranks."

How do I know that Andy will return? Because I know he is a man of his word. If he said thirty years, then thirty years it will be. So when will the exact date of his return be? When I say so. Kind of bold of me? Not really. You see, I'm the only one that Andy would allow to produce his shows. When I feel the time is right, I will pick a date, and that date will become the most anticipated showbiz event in our lifetime. Just think of it—finally the public will see for themselves how Andy looks nowadays and hear from his own lips what he's been up to for the last thirty years. An extraordinary evening!

*   *   *

Being dropped by SNL gave Andy a real situation that he could work material out of. He would not hide the fact that he was let go from SNL, which is how most performers would handle it—just downplay it. How embarrassing. Not Andy. Like I said before, he went for the embarrassment. He would mine it like gold. He would yell it from the rooftop: "Look, everybody—I've been fired from SNL. *Taxi* has been canceled. My wife has left me and took the kids. [He had no wife.] My career is over." Once again, looking for that reality to sink his teeth into, the perfect masochistic role to play out. And if it was real, so much the better. He'd be a loser again—pathetic, a street wino. Nothing to live for. Just get sick and die. What FUN! What a brilliant way to walk away from it all. A perfect ending to a perfectly destroyed career. Talk about punk—Andy Kaufman is the godfather of punk.

Oddly, as he played out this scenario, I had the feeling that there was something eerily familiar about it. I had seen this all played out before. But where? And then one day it hit me—it was Andy's original Bombing Routine. But this time, instead of Foreign Man breaking down and crying *onstage,* he breaks down crying on *national TV.* It's what Jeff Conaway said about Andy's being fired from *Taxi*: "He *wanted* to be fired." The same was true when Tony Clifton poured eggs over Dinah Shore's head. He wanted the studio security guards to drag him off the lot. Then he gets all America crazy with the wrestling. George even warns him he's "killing his career." That makes him want to do it more. He then pushes Dick Ebersol to have him voted off SNL. He was doing everything in his power to bring it all crashing down around him. It's the Bombing Routine revisited. It worked before and it will work again. He'd start to die (just like he did on stage) and then just when they were about ready to bring down the curtain, he'd pull it out of the crapper and win them back over. What was it the maharishi said when Andy asked him, "What's the secret of comedy?" TIMING! And how about when I would give him a hard time about telling people like John Moffitt and Mimi that he was going to fake his death? He'd just shrug it off and say, "That'll all work out in the long run." THE LONG RUN. The long run meant THIRTY YEARS! That brilliant, metaphysical motherfucker had it figured out from day one. It was TIMING. He set up the premise and waited thirty years for the fucking punch line. Kaufman's coming back! I'd stake my reputation on it.

*   *   *

Nothing beats death like immortality. A chance to poke the old Grim Reaper in the eye and send him back to where he came from. If you've ever been in a near-fatal accident or know anyone who has, then you will know this to be true: the moment you know you are out of harm's way, you breathe a deep sigh of relief and then laugh! Who says you can't laugh at death?—Andy Kaufman is!

So in the end, Andy decided to take on the Holy Grail of all topics—Death itself! The one thing everyone's been told since they were little kids never to joke about—DEATH! And perhaps by his faking his death, he forces us to laugh about it. Poke that corpse to see if it's a dead Andy or a wax Andy.

But then of course there are those who won't be laughing when he returns. Certainly the insurance companies that paid out the death benefits won't. The criminal-justice system isn't going to be rolling in the aisle. What about members of his own family? After all, it was Andy's death that contributed greatly to Mrs. Kaufman's own death. She was grief-stricken, something I warned him about time and time again.

How about the media? Will they find it funny? What will Dick Ebersol think about this one? "It's not funny."

And how about Lynne, the love of his life? All those years without him? Think of the family they could have had together. All the tears she shed. Was it really worth it?

And how about me? All the wonderful shows we could have mounted in a span of thirty years. All the missed opportunities for TV and film. All the laughs we didn't have.

Some people are going to be mad at you, Andy. You'd better be prepared for that and have a well-thought-out statement to read. You have a lot of explaining to do.

As for me, I'm going to laugh my ass off. After all, you and I have the same sick sense of humor. As for the others who don't, remember what we always said: "If they can't take a joke, fuck 'em!" After all, it was never about them, anyway. It was about us. Just us. Andy, if you show up for any one person, show up for me. "If you make only one person happy," make it me. Besides, if you don't show, I will be humiliated beyond belief. I'd never be able to show my face in Hollywood again. That's why I know you'll be there. You don't want to see that happen to your Dr. Zmudee.

*   *   *

Before Andy took that leap into mortality, he had one more card to play. And if that panned out, he was prepared to call the whole "dying routine" off. It was film. Film is where Andy really belonged in the first place, for in film he could be as esoteric as he wanted to be. He watched all the masters—Truffaut, Fellini, Wertmuller, Kurosawa. He even was thinking of doing a remake of *Miracle in Milan,* a film by Vittorio De Sica, with Andy playing Toto, the magical Christ-like figure. No more of these silly sitcoms with laugh tracks. Film had the potential to save him, but it was tricky. One misstep and a film career could be over in a minute. The right script would have to be found, developed, fine-tuned, and then produced, directed, acted, and edited with great care.

He and I felt we had found that vehicle in *The Tony Clifton Story*, written by Andy and myself and to be produced by George Shapiro and Howard West. Director John Landis, who was hot as all hell with such hits as *Animal House* and *The Blues Brothers*, persuaded Universal Studios executives Ned Tanen, Thom Mount, Sean Daniel, and a new recruit, Bruce Berman, to give Andy and me a "housekeeping deal" and develop the project. Soon all the nightmares of Andy's television career began to fade away as he and I wrote something he believed in and loved. He was back in his sandbox having fun. The studio liked our first draft a lot and wanted some changes, which we were happy and eager to provide. Finally the script was ready to be handed to the head of the studio, Ned Tanen, for his comments. *The Tony Clifton Story* would put Andy back on top in a new medium and save him from the gallows or at least thirty years in exile. So we crossed our fingers and hoped for the best.

But then disaster struck. It was a film called *Heartbeeps* and had stinker written all over it. How do I know? Because I was told this by three or four Universal secretaries who had read the script and said, "Danger, Will Robinson!" It's common knowledge that the secretarial pool of every major studio knows the hits and misses before everybody else. While sitting around screening phone calls for execs and doing their nails, they read every script the studio has in development. They shouted out a warning to us to stay as far away from this turkey as possible. What made matters worse, however, was that the studio was dangling the co-starring role to Andy, with a sizable payday. His leading lady would be Bernadette Peters. This was Kaufman's big shot as a movie star. I pleaded with him not to do it. It was a character he knew nothing about and a script that lay there like a lox. What made matters worse, the director, Allan Arkush, was green as all hell. I begged Andy to pass on it, knowing that if it failed, no way would they do *Clifton.*

Unfortunately, he accepted the role and the good-size payday that went along with it. Biggest mistake of his life. Both Bernadette and Andy were playing robots. They had major problems with the makeup from Day 1. The metallic robot-like prosthetic pieces on their faces restricted any facial expressions whatsoever. They could only act with their eyes. Besides that, application of the makeup took too long. Andy would arrive on the set by 7:00 a.m., sit in the makeup chair, and not be camera-ready till two or three in the afternoon. Ridiculous. And remember, Andy had written in his contract that he "had to have time to meditate." This held up the production even longer and started to build up resentment with the studio and crew, in that Andy was causing them to fall behind. What's more, according to George Shapiro, Allan Arkush, the kid director, didn't want Andy or Bernadette to be funny, as he looked at the work as a "sensitive love story." Everybody's thinking, "Why have Kaufman and Peters in the first place if you don't want them to be funny?" Soon the production soured. Andy hated it. Worse than *Taxi.*

The only relief for him came in the form of … (what else?) … hookers. In this case, a lot of hookers. An executive at Universal (who shall remain nameless) came up with the idea that if you can't beat them, join them, and devised a "deal" with Andy that if he arrived at the set two days in a row on time, a young prostitute would be waiting for him in his Winnebago. Actually the idea had merit, and George at first supported the Universal exec's plan. The idea died, however, when the line producer said "money for call girls" wasn't coming out of his budget. And then studio executive Thom Mount got wind of the plan. He exploded and said, "No way. If anyone found out, the studio would have a major scandal on their hands," and nixed the whole thing. Meanwhile, for the first time Andy was on time two days running, until they had to tell him the deal was a no-go. After that, he went back to being late.

The film finally wrapped and everyone was anxiously waiting for it to come out. Would Andy be a movie star and then finally we could get the *Clifton* movie made? I had an uneasy feeling about it all. Soon it was confirmed. They screened a rough cut for studio executives. They hated it! Perhaps they were wrong. Maybe the public would like it. The film opened on December 18, 1981. It received some of the worst reviews in film history. And just like that—poof! Andy Kaufman's film career was over before it began. Andy, not to miss a golden opportunity to air his dirty laundry and embarrassment on national TV, went on *Letterman* and offered a refund to anyone who paid to see *Heartbeeps*.

The *Clifton* picture was off and we were asked to vacate our bungalow on the Universal lot posthaste. No other movie studio would touch him. George tried to save face by telling us that ratings for *Taxi* were at an all time low and that's the reason Universal didn't want to do *Clifton* any more. Bullshit! Everyone knew *Heartbeeps* was the reason.

Eventually, Andy's concerts dried up totally. I needed work. Luckily, the guys at Universal who liked me and my writing abilities soon hired me back (without Andy) to write another project for them, *The P.T. Barnum Story*, that would star John Belushi and be directed by John Landis.

Now the plan to fake his death became Andy's main occupation. There was nothing else to live for. Once he found his "body double," the clock started counting down. Now it was simply a question of pretending to die at the same time the body double really did.

In the days of the golden age of wrestling, most of its audience believed it to be real. Wrestling stars of the time would cut their foreheads with hidden razor blades, unbeknownst to the audience, and bleed profusely, with the blood flowing down over their entire faces. Kaufman needed to do the same. In his case, instead of blood, it would be the "cough." He would significantly place it on the right TV show at the right time. It sounded phony as all hell to me, but then again, I saw it coming. He kept doing it, every time more frequently, until his friends would all say to him, "Andy, you should really look into that." He'd say, "I hope it isn't cancer!"

I would get mad at him when he would tell people that. "Jesus, Andy, you can't tell people you have cancer before you're even diagnosed with it." And then when he supposedly did have it, he'd forget at times to act like he did. He almost blew it with his own brother, Michael. When Michael heard that Andy was very sick, he flew out to the West Coast to see him. Michael was shocked at how bad off Andy looked. His weight had dropped significantly and he couldn't talk or walk. Miraculously, the very next day Andy was back to his old self. In fact, a few days after that he was once again driving himself around in his own car. When Michael asked, "How can this be? Just yesterday he couldn't even move," he was told it was the "medication." Michael bought the answer hook, line, and sinker. I kept telling Andy, "You better stay in character or somebody is going to call you on the phony baloney." After my warning, he became more conscious of how to act. Still, every once in a while he slipped. But as time went on, as the consummate actor, he was impeccable and totally convincing as the "dying man."

I don't believe he paid off any doctor to go along with the deception. He didn't have enough money to do that. Besides, doctors do have ethics. At least I want to believe so. He did pay off the secondary people, the working stiffs in the back rooms who didn't get paid diddly-squat, some people who could easily switch a different X-ray to a different file and make themselves a grand. He had successfully pulled the same thing off at a well-known hospital years before, when he faked hurting his neck. He substituted someone else's X-ray with severely compacted vertebrae for his own. He figured it worked before and it would work again.

At the time of his death, about 85 percent of the public's first response was "bullshit." It's like the neck injury with the wrestling. It's a prank. Now remember what made the neck injury believable was the fact that he wore the stupid neck brace for six months. Then people thought, "Well, he must have been injured. Who would wear a neck brace for that long?" Same was true about faking his death. The longer he could stay out of sight, the more believable it would become. The only reason people believe he is dead is that he hasn't been seen for thirty years.

No matter how thorough Andy was in pulling off his death, he did make critical mistakes. Luckily nobody picked up on them. First, he never ever acted as if he was really going to die. Ever. I've lost a lot of loved ones. When someone is going to die, there's either fear or defiance in his or her eyes. Andy's eyes possessed neither. In fact, there was almost a comfortable nonchalance. Talk to anyone who knew him at the time, and they'll all tell you the same thing: "He never acted like a guy who was about to meet his maker." Lynne has always stated that at no time did Andy believe he was dying. Why is that, Lynne? The answer is obvious: because he knew he wasn't.

Second, what about that daughter of his, Maria, whom he never met? Even though he was supposedly dying, he never once tried to seek her out. Who wouldn't want to see his own child before he died? Most people do. But Andy couldn't care less. Why? Because he knew he really wasn't dying and therefore didn't do the things that normal dying people would do, like seeing their long-lost child for the first and last time.

Still, he got away with both of these mistakes. As for his close friends who said that he wasn't taking his dying seriously, they would only scratch their heads and think, "Andy's always been crazy. So why shouldn't he also be crazy about his own death?" Andy was crazy ... crazy as a fox!

Let me repeat this because it's very important: The only reason people believe Andy is dead is because of time. It's been thirty years now. Thirty years. Who could possibly pull a prank off that would take thirty years? No one. Therefore, he *must* be dead. The answer is no, he isn't dead. He just took thirty years to get you to believe he's dead. Remember what he did with *The Great Gatsby*?

He just didn't read fifteen minutes of the book to the audience. He read the whole damn book. Three hours later, there would be five people left in the theater. In the case of faking his death, it's not three hours but thirty years. Beyond brilliant! He was building a cathedral. Cathedrals don't take six years. In some cases they take 600 years to build. He's spent thirty-four years planning and pulling off his faked death and over that time I've kept my mouth shut about it. Why? It was my job. But no more. He said thirty years, and I'm going to hold him to that. It's time for him to come back home and embrace his friends and family. He's pulled off the impossible. He's put in the years and built his own cathedral to himself. Andy, it's standing-ovation time.

*   *   *

This is one of the final discussions Andy and I had on faking his death, which by now we jokingly referred to as "the dying routine." I knew that liftoff would happen soon, as his tone by now had become quite serious and introspective.

B: THIRTY YEARS?! That's a lifetime.

A: I know.

B: So I'm going to be out of work for thirty years?

A: I can leave you some money?

B: No, don't do that. They'll trace it to you and I'll probably end up going to jail as a conspirator to insurance fraud. Besides, Sean and Bruce at Universal are big supporters.

A: How's that Belushi script coming along?

B: *P.T. Barnum*? I'm researching the hell out of it. You know he's the original prankster and John

Belushi is the spitting image of him. John Landis is off in London shooting some werewolf movie. [This would be *An American Werewolf in London*.] When he returns, I'll give him a first draft and then we'll see where things stand.

A: They hate me at Universal. You were right. I never should have done *Heartbeeps*. It killed *The Tony Clifton Story*.

B: Hey, no use crying over spilled milk and cookies. So what are you going to do about Lynne?

A: She's an artist. She understands me as much as you do.

B: Understand? Andy, the woman's in love with you. You're just going to leave for thirty years?

A: I've been thinking about it a lot, and it's probably better if she really thinks I'm dead. Then she can go on with her life. Or maybe I should get her to hate me. That might be the kindest way to go.

B: Are you sure you want to do this? It's beginning to sound pretty fucked up.

A: Bob, it's who I am and what I do. Nothing could ever top it. I've given it great thought. Besides, I'm getting psyched. I'm starting an entire new life.

B: What about your family?

A: There's this guy in the TM movement. His name's John Gray. He's brilliant. He holds these therapy sessions for families. I've been thinking about signing me and my family up for some. I'll do it when it's looking like I don't have long to live. I want to get a lot off my chest. I'm thinking I'll invite George to them also. It'll be therapeutic for everybody, myself included. It'll help everybody get through my loss better. It'll be closure. I'm not going to just leave everybody hanging.

B: Aren't you going to miss performing?

A: I'm going to keep performing.

B: How you going to do that when everyone knows how you look?

A: I'll do children's parties. That's how I started out. I'd love to go back to it. I'd wear clown makeup, like Clarabelle did on *The Howdy Doody Show*. Nobody would know it's me. Maybe I'll get one of those little clown cars to drive around in. I'll call myself something stupid like "Zany Clowny."

B: Zany Clowny!

[*We laughed, and then I got serious.*]

B: Are you ever going to call me?

[*The phone went silent for the longest time and then he spoke.*]

A: I better not. They'll probably be listening in ... but things can change.

Ever since he left us, no matter what city I'm in, I always check the local Yellow Pages under "Children's Entertainment," more out of routine than anything else, to see if there's ever a "Zany Clowny" listed.

It may be wishful thinking on my part, but I'd like to believe that he told his mother about faking his death and had her swear to secrecy not to tell any other family members. I say this because of something Michael Kaufman said his mom said to him a full year before Andy was ever diagnosed with cancer:

"She said to me, 'Poor Andy.' At the time, I had no idea what she meant or why she said it … Years later, I just chalked it up to be a 'mother's instinct' that she knew he didn't have long to live."

Mother's instinct? Déjà vu? One thing Janice Kaufman knew for certain, as only a mother could, was that once her son Andy made up his mind to do something, nothing or no one could talk him out of it, and he would follow it through, as Stanley Kaufman put it:

> … with the utmost precision. Audiences might think what he did was spontaneous—it wasn't. Total control all the time. Premeditated, calculated, he rehearsed constantly. My wife and I were astonished one day when we opened up the neighborhood Penny Saver and there was an ad that Andy was running as a "Children's Party Performer" at $25 an hour. We knew nothing about it. Andy had spent his own money taking it out and designed it himself. He was only nine years old … Nine! … Pretty entrepreneurial at that age.

CHAPTER 9

Andy Will Be Back

A ndy, as a child, was not only the performer on the shows in his room to the imaginary camera; he was also the network executive. Each show lasted either thirty minutes or an hour. They were completely different. They included comedy, music, drama, horror, cartoons, games, soap operas, etc. Andy would also select the products that would be sold during the commercial breaks. The program was daily, and young Andy would rush home from school every day, making sure his programming would begin promptly at 4:00 p.m. Stanley Kaufman could only stand outside his son's room and listen through the door. To him, it had to be sheer madness. As Andy got older and the network in his head grew, he needed more studio space. By now the Kaufman family was forced to move upstairs to the second floor of the house, where they continued to live so Andy could use the entire downstairs for his imaginary telecasts. Greg Sutton, a close childhood friend of Andy's, would say, "It was the strangest house to visit. Andy's entire family would be sequestered on the second floor. We'd hang out on the first floor, where Andy had total run of the place." Andy made it quite clear to Stanley that he needed his space or he threatened to move out of the home altogether. To prove that he was serious, he actually left home and lived in the city park for over a month, sleeping underneath a park bench in a sleeping bag. Stanley, who feared for Andy's safety, acquiesced and gave Andy the bottom half of the family dwelling just to keep him at home. So like everything else in his life, when Andy made the decision to do something, there was no turning back. This time it would be his death, pulled off with "the utmost precision."

*   *   *

Here now is a blow-by-blow account of how I believe Andy Kaufman faked his own death. Although his final methodology can only be conjecture on my part, it is based on numerous conversations I had with him over a period of three years on how to do it. I want to state for the record that I constantly reminded Andy that what he was planning on doing was illegal and that I could not help him, as I did not want to be implicated in criminal activity. At the same time, I told him that if he did pull it off, it would truly be one of the most remarkable events in show-business history. I also would remind him that to pull it off successfully, he would have to convince even me that he in fact had died.

So how did he convince me? *Time.* For the first four, six, maybe seven years, I was convinced that he faked it. Then eight, nine, ten, eleven, twelve years in, I started to doubt. Ten years after that, twenty-three years in, I figured I'd have to be insane to believe he was still alive. I thought he was dead. But not anymore. He faked his death and this is how he did it.

To fake your death, you need to pull off an illusion, very much like a professional magician does. Getting the audiences to believe one thing while in fact something altogether different has happened. Andy had an easier job doing it than a magician because in the case of the magician, an entire audience is closely looking for the trick or gimmick involved to catch the magician. In Andy's case, he only has to fool a handful of people into thinking he's sick and then dying. And remember, unlike an entire audience, these few people are not even looking for a deception to take place, which makes Kaufman's task a whole lot easier than, say, David Copperfield's. Still, the fewer people around the better. This is why he was incensed with Lynne when she contacted his family behind his back to come out and see him in the hospital. Now he had four more pairs of eyes to deal with.

Next, just like a magician, Andy needs an accomplice or accomplices to assist him in pulling his illusion off. In this case, he needs someone who is willing to die for him; i.e., someone who is going to die anyway. But for financial gain or to be a part of pulling off this incredible prank (it could be someone who is also a fan of his), someone agrees to act as Kaufman's body double. This body double was found by scouring different cancer treatment facilities in San Francisco. Andy knew they had to be male and be close to his age, but height and eye color had to be exact. Facial structure could be corrected by prosthetic pieces, just like he and I did to make me look like his Clifton. Weight could be controlled by him losing weight to match his double. But most important, the body double had to be dying from something that would take his life in a relatively short amount of time (six months?) and something that could not be cured. God forbid Andy would invest so much time and money only to have the body double get better. Another accomplice would be the body double's loved one or caregiver. He or she would be needed once the body double became too ill to maneuver around on his own, and crucial when the switch would take place. Once those individuals had been found and the financial arrangement had been agreed upon, they were off and running. Or I should say, "off and dying."

Now Andy had five months to get in shape, or more appropriately, get out of shape. He would meet with his body double occasionally, learning to mirror his appearance, speech patterns, gait and attitude as much as he could. Andy would put himself on a strict diet to do just that and copy the "radiation look" to match the double's, which caused hair loss. Andy would either receive radiation himself—remember, he called me once asking, "How much radiation could a healthy body take?"—or simply cosmetically match how the double's hair loss would look. I'm reminded how Jim Carrey quickly lost weight and shaved his entire head to achieve the "dying look" for the film. With a little skin-tone makeup (grayish), Jim was totally believable as a cancer patient with a short time to live. The use of a wheelchair in both cases (Andy's and Jim's) helped in pulling off the illusion. Now that the match up was close enough to fool the average person, and the body double's days were quickly drawing to a close, this is when Andy went to the Philippines for "psychic surgery" as part of the plan to convince the American public that he was really dying. The gruesome photos were leaked to the *National Enquirer* for all to see. When Andy got word that the body double only had a short time to live, he flew back to the States and eventually checked himself into Cedars-Sinai Hospital, all the time monitoring the body double, who was coming closer to the end at some undisclosed location. The second accomplice would be used to stay in communication with Andy and transport the near-death body double to the hospital at just the right time. Another sick person being pushed around in a wheelchair at Cedars-Sinai would hardly be noticed.

And now the critical moment would take place. This is when the "trick" or "switch" takes place. On stage, a magician would mask the switch right before our eyes with a puff of smoke or a beautiful sexy assistant to divert our attention. Andy at the hospital would need a diversion also. Something to divert that handful of his friends and family who gathered around him for the final vigil. Luckily, this final vigil took days, with people walking in and out of Andy's room. A few would leave occasionally (like I did) to go eat, sleep, go to the bathroom, make a phone call, etc. Remember, no more than a minute was needed to accomplish the switch, which took place when everybody had stepped out momentarily. Then the body double would be wheeled in by his accomplice. Andy would then quickly jump out of bed and be replaced. Andy would be put in the wheelchair and, before you could say "Maharishi Mahesh Yogi," be transported out of the building before any family member or friends returned. With the prosthetics already put firmly in place over the body double's face and the matchup being worked on for months, when the guests would filter back into the room, they just assumed it was still Andy in bed … but it wasn't. Andy was transported to another location, where he would have his first real meal in months. When the body double finally succumbed, all gathered around totally believing Andy had died. The corpse was now covered with a sheet and taken down to the morgue. In the middle of the night, the accomplice had one last duty to perform and that was to remove the prosthetic pieces from the corpse. The next day, the body was sent to Nassau Funeral Home in Great Neck for a formal viewing before burial at nearby Beth David cemetery.

When one of Andy's close friends viewed the now mortician-prepared body at the funeral home and commented, "Jesus, it doesn't even look like him," a reply from another well-wisher gathered was simply, "Cancer will do that to you." The illusion is now complete. The body double is safely buried, while the magician takes a thirty-year break, growing his hair back and also a beard, along with gaining as much weight as he can, so he will actually be fat for the first time in his life. As for family and friends who were gathered at the hospital for the death watch (unless they were in on it), I believe they believed they saw Andy wither away and die. What they saw was *Andy* wither away but they saw *someone else* die. Presto change-o!!!

As for the body in the casket at the funeral home in Great Neck, it could be a wax dummy or the body double's. Andy had some distinctive marks on his face, most notably his eyebrows. The body double's eyebrows would have been trimmed to look like Andy's, the same procedure the hair people on *Man on the Moon* did with Jim's eyebrows, or it was wax. I do know that Andy had two sets of facial casts that were given to him. One was from makeup artist Ken Chase, and the other was the mold they did of his face on *Heartbeeps*. After his death, neither mold was ever found among his belongings.

As for the body double's funeral, wouldn't his family have missed his body? I can only speak with some certainty on what Andy himself had told me. When I informed him what he was about to do was illegal and the less I knew about it the better, he complied with my wishes and stopped talking. Therefore, the intricacies of the body double's funeral were unknown to me. If I was to venture a guess, I'd say that the body double's accomplice told the relatives (if there were any) that the body double had died, and his wishes were not to have a large funeral but a simple ceremony where his ashes would be scattered over his favorite spot. Case closed.

There's no doubt that there were many, many other small details involved in accomplishing this, but basically it's not as complicated as it first appears. It is estimated that over 6,000 people fake their deaths annually, over 400 in the U.S. alone. Like any great illusion, the trick is simpler than one can imagine. First he disappears and now, thirty years later, he reappears!

*   *   *

OK, Kaufman, I'm going to end by making you an offer you can't refuse. Since you've been out of commercial entertainment for the last thirty years, and since you had to put out a good sum of money to pull off your death, I'm guessing you may be at the point in your life where you might need funds, if not for yourself then for your wife and new children (if you have any), as I'm sure you're concerned about their futures. Therefore I am willing to offer you $1 million.

Here's how it will work: I have signed a contract with one of the largest concert promoters in the country, HUKA Entertainment. Its CEO, A.J. Niland, has said after you return the first time, within three months he'd like to mount a second massive "coliseum size" event and pay you $1 million.

*   *   *

Andy, I don't have to tell you how big and controversial an event your return will be. My staff and I are already preparing ourselves for a media frenzy and so should you. You should give thought to bringing on board a full-time publicist. (I'm compiling a list for you to choose from.) The day after your return is going to be quite busy, as we will be fielding offers from all media. Certainly the major morning news shows, such as ABC's *Good Morning America,* NBC's *Today,* and *CBS This Morning,* are going to want you to be on. We've been kicking this around and feel that you should keep them at bay at first, and we should focus on the talk shows for an exclusive. We will have *The View, Ellen, 60 Minutes, Dr. Phil,* etc., to choose from, but *60 Minutes* is probably your best bet. And it would help ticket sales if you appeared on it closer to your coliseum event. *Dr. Phil* we can do later. I'm sure he'll take the position that what you did was cruel to those who loved you, and something like this really opens up a whole discussion of death and how we all deal with it. There will be skeptics, since I'm sure you look quite different than you did thirty years ago. So I'd like to have some non-invasive DNA testing taken on your return—just hair and fingernail samples will do. I'm told within ten days we will have the results.

Probably one of the most important phone calls I want to have is a conference call the day after your return with you, me, and Lorne Michaels from SNL, as I'd like you to host SNL. You can do a bit where this time the audience votes Dick Ebersol out of ever producing the show again. We won't be mean about it. Perhaps you and Dick can make up on the air. Like they say, time heals all.

Anyway, all of this is going to be great fun. I mention some of this now so you will have time to consider the possibilities. But then again, I'm sure that you have many ideas along with directions to give since you've had thirty years to think about it. Can't wait to hear them. Now Andy, I fully realize that you might not want any of this. After all, it's your life. You might be a Buddhist monk for all I know, and I totally support your decision either way. But if you do, I'm there for you and have a good staff of people at your disposal.

One of the top agencies in town has already contacted me in hopes of being the first in signing you. They believe your product-endorsement potential can well be in the seven figures the first year alone. They stated, "Andy Kaufman faking his death for thirty years may just be the smartest move an entertainer has ever made. It's right up there with Robert Redford creating his Sundance empire and Paul Newman developing his own food line of Newman's Own. We'd be honored to represent him and take what he and Bob started to the next level."

Andy, I hope you're reading this, and I'd be a liar if I didn't see massive dollar signs at stake. Just keep in mind, every penny that Paul Newman made from his Newman's Own products went directly into his charity programs. You can also alleviate a lot of suffering on this planet by your return. As you know, after you left, I was forced to reinvent myself, as I too became disenchanted with Hollywood and fell into a whole other field quite by accident. With the support of Billy Crystal, Robin Williams, and Whoopi Goldberg, I founded Comic Relief, a nationally recognized major charity. To date we have raised over $80 million for those in need. Andy, Comic Relief is living proof that Hollywood is not all greed.

I've decided that ticket sales for your return will be a fundraiser for Comic Relief. Specifically, I want to raise funds to help save the elephants. Did you know that over 25,000 elephants a year are slaughtered for the illegal ivory trade? Some corrupt African countries actually use their own military helicopters to swoop down upon elephant herds in the middle of the night, and then wearing night goggles, they machine gun the entire herd. Then they land

and cut off the tusks of these gentle giants, some who unfortunately are still alive. The females and youngsters who don't even have tusks are slaughtered along with the rest. Elephants, like humans, are known to mourn their dead. When they return the next day after the slaughter to do so, they too are slain. International crime organizations are running the operation and filtering the profits from the slaughter to finance al-Qaeda to kill Americans. Your return will not only raise funds that evening, but also help bring attention to this issue. It's a shitty world, Kaufman, but your new-born celebrity can bring a lot of attention to some very important issues. To find out more about what's happening to the elephants, I'd suggest going to the International Fund for Animal Welfare (IFAW) website (http://www.ifaw.org/united-states).

I also spoke to a good contact I have over at Universal who totally believes you faked your death and told me that if you do choose to return, Universal will make *The Tony Clifton Story* in a "a New York minute." Wouldn't that be a gas? Do you know that Tony Clifton is now the exact age that we created him to look like over thirty years ago? I.e., we don't have to wear those time-consuming prosthetic pieces, like sagging jowls, anymore to make ourselves look older. We are older. I don't know about you, but I've put on some weight. Maybe you haven't. Probably not, because I'm only guessing that you've maintained your TM and yoga and that would keep you slim. I can't wait to see you again. Actually, I'm quite anxious about it. I'm sure there'll be many tears shed (and some anger), but I'm telling close friends of yours who are planning on attending to keep all of that behind closed doors afterwards. I tell them to remember that you will be appearing for the first time in thirty years in a public forum. So let's keep it light and theatrical at first. Afterwards back in the green room is when you can meet those closest to you and then the tears can flow. I'll also have a private room set up just for you and Lynne. She's totally convinced herself over the years that you died, and possibly of AIDS. She had herself tested and luckily turned up negative. When you show up,

I'm not sure if her mind is going to be able to take it all in. Dr. Joe Troiani suggested I have some trained counselors in attendance just in case some people start freaking out. Do consider saying a few words to the audience that night. Nothing like this has ever been attempted and I just want to be totally prepared for whatever, including "mass hysteria." I'm going to hire three times the security we would normally have, plus a couple of medics with smelling salts. You'll have some die-hard fans present, rest assured. We'll do everything to protect your safety and the safety of your family, if you have one, who you may decide to bring with you. David Letterman is going to have another heart attack when he sees you.

And don't even give a thought to this "gay" issue. Much has changed in thirty years, and unless you've been living under a rock, nobody cares anymore about somebody's sexual preferences. So if you have a significant other nowadays who just happens to be male, Lynne and I would love to meet him. Also be prepared for others showing up who will claim to be you. We have a good way of sorting that out as Lynne has described a certain mole on a certain part of your body that the public has not been privy to. Our security will not allow anyone claiming to be you to be let onstage unless he shows that mole. So don't be offended if you have to take your shirt off and be checked. Lynne said you'll know what she's talking about.

Andy, you've pulled off some crazy stunts in your lifetime, but this one certainly takes the cake. I'm curious to see how or if your philosophy on life has changed. The world has become so terribly materialistic in thirty years, something that I know you struggled not to be a part of, which I know was part of the motivation of your "checking out." Certainly your return, as I just stated, is going to open up countless lucrative deals. I wonder if you're prepared for that. I would strongly advise that you start thinking in terms of a financial adviser. Come the day after your return you will overnight become one of the highest-paid celebrities out there. It would be good for you to have at last a preliminary game plan ready so you can hit the ground running. My staff and I have kicked this around for the last year and have some thoughts on it. I'm hoping that you would like to retain my services as both your writer and producer. If not, no problem. I'll be happy just to see you again, buddy.

I'm going to try my darnedest to get your brother and sister to attend your return. As I've described thus far, the relationship between them and Lynne is at an all-time low. I'm glad on your return you'll be able to straighten everything out, thus there'll be no need for this Andy Kaufman Memorial Trust business.

I can't wait to hear your take on *Man on the Moon.* Lynne doesn't think the film captured you at all. I'm not as harsh, realizing it was an impossible task to begin with, and it has brought a new young audience as a fan base, which you'll experience on your return. I can't wait to have you and Jim Carrey meet. The guy really worked his ass off trying to capture you, so if you didn't like his performance, maybe try to keep it to yourself.

I've contacted two of the three prostitutes who attended your funeral. They will also be there on your return. Both of course are out of the business and now have families of their own. (They're still meditating.) Sadly, the third girl passed away eight years ago due to breast cancer. She gave me a letter to give to you upon your return. She also never gave up hope that you were still alive. She'd call me up every few years around the anniversary of your "death" wanting to know if you were secretly in contact with me. I could honestly say no. When she only had a few months to live, I contacted her and told her a little white lie. I told her that you had contacted me. She was beside herself with joy and said, "I knew it." She died a short time afterward.

And last but not to "be de least" is your own daughter Maria, whom you never met. Kaufman, I swear, she has the exact same eyes as you. I've decided not to invite her to your return. I think that could be a little too much for you and her to handle. I will leave it to you to reach out to her when you're ready. I know you'll be proud of her. She is quite a remarkable woman, married to a great guy named Joe Colonna. She holds no resentment, either against you or her biological mother, for giving her up for adoption. She realized you both were kids yourself at the time, and it was the right thing to do. Andy, she's so proud that you're her dad. And so is her daughter, who soon will be calling you Papu. It's a chance for you to correct an unintentional hurt that happened to you as a child when your grandfather died.

You know there will be ramifications, as I warned you thirty years ago that faking your death is illegal. I've spoken to a couple of lawyers at Mitchell Silberberg & Knupp who feel confident that, under these unusual circumstances, and because they feel you really didn't fake your death for financial gain but rather to exercise your First Amendment right of free expression, all of this could be cleared up by simply repaying those monies paid out with interest (another reason to take the mil). Also I think (and I'm sure you'll agree) that something special should be done for the family of your body double. Without him, you never would have been able to pull any of this off. I'm guessing your body double is in your grave. Upon your return, an exhumation could take place and his body could be returned to his loved ones for a proper burial. His funeral thirty years ago was probably a spreading of his "cremains" (powdered cement), as many victims of cancer would rather their ravaged bodies not be put on display. He truly was a diehard fan of yours and on your return we will take time to recognize his contribution. After all, he gave his life to help pull off the greatest hoax of all time. If his accomplice is still alive, he or she, too, should be recognized.

Kaufman, wait till you hear this: if you think your family is nuts, mine's worse. I get a call from Dr. Troiani. It seems my sister Marilyn and her husband Bob Soraparu called him up "concerned about the state of my mental health." What fueled this was that unfortunately I sent them an early draft of this book and they read it and thought I'd gone off the deep end. As they put it, "With this delusion that Andy's still alive." They think that I'm "in denial of your death" and basically I've gone bananas believing that you're returning. What's worse is they fear when you don't show, I'm going to suffer a total mental collapse and might even harm myself. Can you believe such nonsense? So Marilyn asks Dr. Troiani if there's any way he can submit papers that would force me to go see a shrink. Joe told them the process is called "involuntary commitment for a psychiatric evaluation." Can you believe this bullshit? What makes this even funnier is that Marilyn and Bob weren't aware that Dr. Troiani himself believes you faked your death and you're coming back. Of course he didn't tell them that. He just told them that he'll "look into things." So Andy, you'd better show or my sister and her husband are going to have me thrown into the loony bin! How funny is that? Oh, and get this—Marilyn is the same sister who believes the moon landing was faked.

I just got another call from that agent who's dying to sign you. He said he could get you a quarter million dollars if in your first interview when asked, "What's the first thing you're going to do now that you're back from the dead?" you say, "I'm going to Disneyland!"

And the big question that I'm going to want to know is … was Lynne in on it or not? Some days I think she might have been because she's so good at keeping these things hidden (after all, she's "old school" wrestling), so maybe this "died of AIDS" thinking is just part of her smokescreen to throw off Dr. Zmudee from suspecting her involvement. If she really didn't know and you fooled her like you did everybody else, be prepared for her to be *really* pissed at you. Andy, she deeply loved you. Still does. I know you both had dreams of marriage and everything, and some are going to look at what you did as pretty rotten and mean. And I must admit there's some degree of truth in that, although I do consider the bigger picture. So I'm hoping she was in on this whole thing all along.

Welcome back!

Other Kaufman Books

Was This Man a Genius? by Julie Hecht (Random House, 2001)

Dear Andy Kaufman, I Hate Your Guts! by Lynne Margulies (introduction) (Process, 2009)

Lost in the Funhouse, by Bill Zehme (Delacorte Press, 1999)

Andy Kaufman Revealed! by Bob Zmuda (Little Brown, 1999)
  Out of print—Signed hardcover copies by author available on www.AndyKaufmanReturns.com

Acknowledgments

Bob would like to thank a number of individuals without whose support this book would not have been possible:

First and foremost, my lifelong friend, author, and past publicist, Jodee Blanco, whose inexhaustible devotion to this project knew no bounds, starting with her insistence that BenBella publish this book. (I owe you a dinner date with Richard Gere.)

To Glenn Yeffeth, publisher of BenBella Books, whose last name is impossible to pronounce. Thanks for doing the book and for editing out most of Lynne's and my sour grapes. You've assembled a great team at BenBella, who cheerfully took me through all the publishing steps and never got tired of my asking, "When did you say the deadline is?" They include Brian Buchanan, Jennifer Canzoneri, Sarah Dombrowsky, Alicia Kania, Katie Kennedy, Adrienne Lang, Lindsay Marshall, Jessika Rieck, and Jenna Sampson.

To Mike Miller, who found time between his executive responsibilities with Comic Relief to go through hundreds of pages of my at times undecipherable writing, which only he can somehow manage to read, even when I myself no longer can.

To Dr. Joe Troiani, associate professor of psychology at Adler University, for his psychological insights into both Andy, who he knew personally, and his wealth of knowledge on post traumatic stress syndrome in his role as the founder of the military psychology program at Adler.

To Judd Apatow, who started with Comic Relief over twenty-eight years ago and went on to become one of Hollywood's top writers, producers, and directors, for graciously finding time to write the foreword.

To Phil Davis of Mitchell Silberberg and Knupp, not only my lawyer for over fourteen years, but a good friend who protects me from … what else? … Other lawyers.

To RoseMarie Terenzio and her team, whose professionalism and expertise gave us clear direction on how to deal with the media for such an unprecedented event, and to Brian Gross.

From HUKA Entertainment, Chairman & CEO AJ Niland and Ryan Chavez, VP Tony Clifton Management, who have the balls to book Tony Clifton, stating it's "the greatest act we've ever seen."

To Wally Wingert, a Kaufman/Clifton aficionado extraordinaire, who began as a fan, but now is family. Wally, thanks for bringing the talented Shirley Borchardt to my attention.

To Frank Weimann of Folio who also agented my first book, *Andy Kaufman Revealed!* (Little Brown).

And to Tony Clifton, who keeps us grounded by never letting us forget that "LIFE'S BULLSHIT!"

A special thanks to those other individuals who brought their talent and/or support. They include Terry Badgett, Gabe Bartalos, Dan Funk, Asa Gilmore, Jeremy Johnson, Bill Karmia, Joe Lauer, Steve Levine of ICM, Jeff Margolis, Robyn Nash of Gersh Agency, Susan Patricola, Amy Shoun, Todd Whitman, Jason Doyle, Don and Carol Peterson, and two new members of the family, Addie Daley and Jack Soraparu.

I am especially thankful to my good friends Dennis Hof, Suzette, Domino, Sophie, and all the staff and girls of the Moonlite Bunny Ranch in Carson City, Nevada. And Ruby, my neighbor's dog, who demands that I stop writing and take her for walks.

And lastly, to Carrie Badgett, Richard Crowe, and Bill "the Moose" Skowron, who may no longer be with us but whose support and inspiration I still feel.

Lynne wishes to acknowledge:

My brother Johnny Legend, who introduced me to Andy; my beloved husband Lon Osgood who, all these years after Andy's passing, has given me back the joy for life and love; and of course, Andy himself.

Thanks for the short, wild roller coaster ride, Andy! Miss you.

About the Authors

A ndy Kaufman and his writing partner, **Bob Zmuda**, changed the worlds of comedy and performance in the 1970s, showing fans and friends alike a determination to follow put-ons into territory no one had ever even considered "comic" before. Their fervor was so intense that when Kaufman passed away suddenly in 1984, it seemed as if his death had been staged, with the reveal soon to come.

Zmuda met Kaufman in 1974, when Zmuda was a struggling comic himself. Soon he began writing for Andy until his (supposed) death in '84. Bob also wrote briefly for Rodney Dangerfield and was the late, great Sam Kinison's producer, "another gifted provocateur," said Zmuda.

For nearly thirty years, Bob Zmuda has been the driving force behind one of America's most beloved charities, Comic Relief, probably best recognized for their telethons on HBO hosted by Robin Williams, Whoopi Goldberg, and Billy Crystal. As president and founder, he and his fellow comedians have raised over $80 million for those in need.

A Grammy nominee and Emmy Award winner, Bob is also a bestselling author. His book *Andy Kaufman Revealed!* made top 10 lists nationwide. Two-time Academy Award–winning director Milos Forman said, "I was so fascinated by the melding of Zmuda and Kaufman's minds that I spent two years of my life making a movie about them, *Man on the Moon*." The film starred Jim Carrey as Kaufman and Paul Giamatti as Zmuda. Zmuda also coexecutive produced the film with Danny DeVito and Jersey Films.

On television, Bob has hosted several series for Comedy Central and A&E. His television appearances include *Saturday Night Live, Late Show with David Letterman, Jimmy Kimmel Live, The Oprah Winfrey Show,* and all the Comic Relief telecasts. His acting credits include *Punchline, Batman Forever, Man on the Moon, D.C. Cab* (which he also wrote), and *The Number 23,* again with Jim Carrey.

For the last few years, Zmuda has been producing Kaufman's alter ego, international singing sensation Tony Clifton, to sold-out audiences. He is currently working on mounting the largest star-studded fund-raiser ever for endangered wildlife worldwide.

Lynne Margulies, artist and filmmaker, was Andy Kaufman's partner, caretaker, and the love of his life until his death from lung cancer in 1984. Courtney Love portrayed Margulies in the Kaufman biopic *Man on the Moon,* starring Jim Carrey. During the film's production, Margulies worked closely with Carrey, giving him rare insight into the human side of Andy Kaufman. Margulies teaches fine art at the Academy of Art University in San Francisco. She is the codirector of the documentary film *I'm from Hollywood,* which chronicles Kaufman's foray into the world of professional wrestling. Her latest art project is *The Book of Steve,* a four-foot by three-foot book which tells the story of her brother's descent into mental illness. Margulies, her musician husband, and their eight cats live on the Oregon coast.